Looking to Nature

Exploring a Modern Way
of Being
Spiritual Without the Supernatural

Todd Macalister

APOCRYPHILE
PRESS

Apocryphile Press
1700 Shattuck Ave #81
Berkeley, CA 94709
www.apocryphilepress.com

Please join our mailing list at
www.apocryphilepress.com/free
We'll keep you up-to-date on all our new releases,
and we'll also send you a FREE BOOK.
Visit us today!

"I cannot conceive of a God who rewards and punishes
his creatures, or has a will of the type of which
we are conscious in ourselves.

An individual who should survive his physical death
is also beyond my comprehension,
nor do I wish it otherwise …

Enough for me the mystery of the eternity of life,
and the inkling of the marvelous structure of reality,
together with the single-hearted endeavor
to comprehend a portion, be it ever so tiny,
of the reason that manifests itself in nature."

— ALBERT EINSTEIN —

"There is a soul at the center of nature,
and over the will of every man …

It has so infused its strong enchantment into nature,
that we prosper when we accept its advice …"

— RALPH WALDO EMERSON —

Contents

Introduction

"A religion ... that stressed the magnificence of the universe
as revealed by modern science,
might be able to draw forth reserves of reverence and awe
hardly tapped by the conventional faiths.
Sooner or later, such a religion will emerge."

— CARL SAGAN

The process Carl Sagan predicted has begun. This hasn't resulted in "a religion." But it has led to something related – where, as involvement in traditional religion is declining, many are exploring ways that a spiritual sense can be grounded in the natural world.

No one believes nothing. We all have a sense of what seems possible and real, and why things happen as they do. And even if it is noticed no more frequently than at a funeral or the birth of a child, we all – at times, and in our own ways – can be spiritual or religious*.

But, for those of us who can't imagine an active personal God, what might we look to as a focus when we consider religious questions, or as we cope with loss or are moved by the mysteries and wonders of being alive?

As it shows a vast and ancient cosmos and amazing beauty and forms of life, nature can spark feelings of awe, appreciation, and caring.

As the creative ordered force that enables us to exist and causes things to be as they are, nature seems worth trying to understand, as best we can.

And, as it can help us find a sense of connection, purpose, meaning, and a foundation for morals and values, looking to nature can offer some of the benefits that many have long sought and gained from religions.

Over the past century, and increasingly in recent decades, a number of philosophers and theologians have been exploring the implications of nature-based spirituality. They often discuss this from "religious naturalist" perspectives, where religious perceptions can be understood, and religious questions can be considered, in ways that fit with a naturalist view (where all is seen as being due to natural processes, with nothing supernatural involved). At the same time, as biologists, physicists, astronomers, and other scientists may be deeply moved by exploring the workings of nature, and as nonacademic folks may be moved by personal experiences in natural settings, we may come to share a view John Muir described – that ...

"In our best times everything turns into religion,
all the world seems a church and the mountains altars."

Many who don't see themselves as religious, in traditional ways, can recognize examples of this – where in a pine grove or by the sea or in some other special place, we can get away for a while from the bustle of everyday life and be prompted to notice things that matter. Many see in these moments examples of some of the best this world can be. And, as we also observe the destructive power of storms and cycles of seasons and life and death, we receive lessons and reminders of the limits in our lives and how all is interconnected.

Looking to nature as a spiritual focus traces back to ancient times. It remains central in a number of traditions, and it offers perspectives that can be valuable as part of our responses to modern challenges.

This can contribute to reconciling conflict between science and religion.

It can expand options in ways of considering Big Questions.

At a time when many have little interest in attending weekly services, it can encourage self-directed exploration and expression, and a focus on personal versus institutional ways of being religious.

And, at a time of rapid change – when explosions in human population and technology have caused destruction of ecosystems, extinctions, changes in climate, and other problems, looking to nature can point to common ground in a belief and value that can be shared by all – that the natural world, which gave birth to us and sustains us, is essential; and in the eyes of many, is sacred.

This view can give emotional and spiritual, as well as practical reasons, to care for and preserve natural environments.

An overview of the coming pages

This book gives an overview of what it can mean to look to nature as a focus of attention. It shows topics that can be considered, ideas of influential teachers, and a range of views that have been discussed. It also points to additional resources, including emerging groups, for those who would like to learn more.

Part 1: A Natural Sense of Ourselves and Our World describes aspects of a naturalist worldview that can prompt insights and responses. It starts broadly – with the origin of and the natural forces in the cosmos. Then it looks more closely, here on Earth, at what it means to be alive, to be human, and to be religious. It points to aspects of nature and human nature that differ from traditional views, and it discusses how, as this shows a beautiful, ordered, interconnected world where life can be seen as sacred, a naturalist view can serve as a foundation from which to consider religious questions.

Part 2: Practices looks at types of things that those who look to nature may do – to learn and grow, help or heal, and put values into practice. It shows how – occasionally or regularly, alone or in groups – we can spend time in nature or with art, community, meditation, rituals, or study, and how these and other traditional and original activities can contribute to our lives.

Part 3 looks at **Questions and Challenges** that can come with this approach. Some involve wrapping our heads around aspects of naturalist views (for example, how we consider ourselves as biological beings). Some other questions can relate to non-traditional ways of being religious.

A **Wrap-up** ties this all together to review what it can mean to look to nature, and how this may contribute to each of us personally, and to our cultures, and to efforts to preserve natural environments.

An **Appendix** provides additional detail on some topics, and a **References and Resources** section points to books and other materials that contributed to views discussed in this book and can be used to explore and learn more.

This approach of looking to nature can be of interest in different ways from varied perspectives.

4

For those who have a spiritual sense but are not attracted to traditional religion, it provides a framework for responding to the wonders and challenges of life in ways that fit with a modern understanding.

For those who see themselves as atheist or secular, it can provide a way of seeing what it can mean to be "religious" that isn't based on institutions, and shift focus from the rejection of traditional approaches to considering what we *do* believe.

For those aligned with established religions, it can expand ways of drawing from the best of modern knowledge and ancient wisdom.

And for those who may be suspicious of approaches that reject aspects of traditional religions, it will show how "nonbelievers" can be spiritual and "good without God". Becoming familiar with this view can enable critique of what this is, rather than demonizing it or fearing misconceptions.

This orientation is not for everyone. But for some it offers a framework that, better than other options, suits our ways of exploring spiritual questions. And for all, it can be worthwhile to know what this is.

*   *Throughout this book, the terms "spiritual" and "religious" are used in ways that acknowledge some overlap in the range of definitions and connotations for these terms.*
    One distinction is that "spiritual" is used mainly in relation to individual perceptions, attitudes and responses, while "religious" can include both this personal sense of being spiritual plus alignment with some of what is done or believed by a group.
    Additional perspectives are discussed in several parts of this book.

Part 1:
A Natural Sense of Ourselves and Our World

This part of the book describes naturalist ways of responding to age-old questions – "What are we?" "How did things come to be?" and "Why do things happen as they do?" It gives an overview of a worldview that is grounded in science and informed by insights from modern and ancient literature, mythology, philosophy, psychology, and other perspectives from the humanities and the arts.

Part 1 begins at the beginning, with the modern story of Origins. Then it moves from broad to more narrow and personal, with chapters on:

Ways of the World
Life
Being Human
Being Religious

Each chapter begins by describing aspects of what can be understood through methods of science, and each concludes with "Reflections" on the spiritual implications of these views.

Origins

"In the beginning (if there was such a thing),
God created Newton's laws of motion
together with the necessary masses and forces.
That is all …
all events, including the actions of mankind,
are determined by laws of nature."

— ALBERT EINSTEIN

All cultures have stories of how the world and its people came to be. Each has a mythic quality that orients us in the grand scheme of all that is. The story tells us what we are and it gives a foundation for considering what we should do.

Genesis 1 has inspired and grounded cultures for millennia. But, in the twentieth century, a different story took form.

This shows an expanding universe, tracing back to a "Big Bang," when a massive expansion of energy led, over time, to formation of galaxies and stars and our solar system and planet.

It shows the formation of Earth and the transformation of its atmosphere and continents.

It shows life beginning as single cells, then, with natural selection, progressing to algae and plants, and to fish, amphibians, reptiles, and mammals in complex ecosystems.

It shows humans evolving from earlier forms of primates, and progressing from hunter/gatherer groups to lives as farmers and factory workers and computer technicians.

This twentieth-century story is well-grounded in science. Although some details remain topics of debate, the broad picture has been widely accepted by cultures and religions worldwide.

This shows a beautiful, intricate, vulnerable world, teeming with life and types of intelligence. It frames an understanding of our nature and our place, in context with other beings on Earth and forces in the cosmos.

Several questions have been asked.

How did this all begin?
What was present before the Big Bang?
Why is there something, rather than nothing?

Answers have been offered, but some of the concepts are hard to grasp and a number of things remain unknown. But a central point remains – that this could, and through naturalist eyes did, all occur due to natural processes. As Steven Hawking put it, "It is not necessary to invoke God to ... set the Universe going." "Because there is a law like gravity, the Universe can and will create itself from nothing."

The modern story

The modern origins story is familiar to people around the world. But, as a central part of a naturalist view, it bears retelling. The version below was written by Carl Sagan.

"For unknown ages after the explosive outpouring of matter and energy of the Big Bang, the Cosmos was without form. There were no galaxies, no planets, no life. Deep, impenetrable darkness was everywhere, hydrogen atoms in the void.

Here and there denser accumulations of gas were imperceptibly growing, globes of matter were condensing – hydrogen raindrops more massive than suns. Within these globes of gas was first kindled the nuclear fire latent in matter. A first generation of stars was born, flooding the Cosmos with light. There were in those times not yet any planets to receive the light, no living creatures to admire the radiance of the heavens.

Deep in the stellar furnaces the alchemy of nuclear fusion created heavy elements, the ashes of hydrogen burning, the atomic building materials of future planets and lifeforms.

Massive stars soon exhausted their stores of nuclear fuel. Rocked by colossal explosions, they returned most of their substance back into the thin gas from which they had once condensed. Here in the dark lush clouds between the stars, new raindrops made of many elements were forming, later generations of stars being born. Nearby, smaller raindrops grew, bodies far too little to ignite the nuclear fire, droplets in the interstellar mist on their way to form the planets. Among them was a small world of stone and iron, the early Earth.

Congealing and warming, the Earth released the methane, ammonia, water and hydrogen gases that had been trapped within, forming the primitive atmosphere and the first oceans. Starlight from the Sun bathed and warmed the primeval Earth, drove storms, generated lightning and thunder. Volcanoes overflowed with lava. These processes disrupted molecules of the primitive atmosphere; the fragments fell back together again into more and more complex forms, which dissolved in the early oceans.

After a time the seas achieved the consistency of a warm, dilute soup. Molecules were organized, and complex chemical reactions driven, on the surface of clays. And one day a molecule arose that quite by accident was able to make crude copies of itself out of the other molecules in the broth. As time passed, more elaborate and more accurate self-replicating molecules arose. Those combinations best suited to further replication were favored by the sieve of natural selection. Those that copied better produced more copies. And the primitive oceanic broth gradually grew thin as it was consumed by and transformed into complex condensations of self-replicating organic molecules. Gradually, imperceptibly, life had begun.

Single-celled plants evolved, and life began to generate its own food. Photosynthesis transformed the atmosphere. Sex was invented. Once free-living forms banded together to make a complex cell with specialized functions. Chemical receptors evolved, and the Cosmos could taste and smell. One-celled organisms evolved into multicellular colonies, elaborating their various parts into specialized organ systems. Eyes and ears evolved, and now the Cosmos could see and hear.

Plants and animals dissolved that the land could support life. Organisms buzzed, crawled, scuttled, lumbered, glided, flapped, shimmied, climbed and soared. Colossal beasts thundered through the steaming jungles. Small creatures emerged, born live instead of in hard-shelled containers, with a fluid like the early oceans coursing through their veins. They survived by swiftness and cunning.

And then, only a moment ago, some small arboreal animals scampered down from the trees. They became upright and taught themselves the use of tools, domesticated other animals, plants, and fire and devised language. The ash of stellar alchemy was now emerging into consciousness. At an ever-accelerating pace, it invented writing, cities, art and science, and sent space-ships to the planets and the stars.

These are some of the things that hydrogen atoms do, given fifteen billion years of cosmic evolution."

Reprinted with permission from *Cosmos*.
Random House. 1980. pages 337-338.

Origins and Evolution – a Timeline						
Big Bang	Earth	Cyanobacteria		Fish Plants	Mammals Reptiles	Humans
13.8	4.5	3.5		500	250	0.150
	Billion years ago			Million years ago		

Reflections

The modern story of origins sparks a sense of wonder, with time tracing back almost 14 billion years and distances beyond what we can imagine. It shows that we live on an ordinary planet, circling an average star, among many trillions of stars in the cosmos. On this tiny planet, humans are one among several millions of species. In the scale of time, we emerged just a moment ago.

It is hard, from this perspective, to see ourselves as the focus of all that is.

The modern view sees the Earth as an oasis – a tiny pale blue dot amid the vast cold reaches of space. In the eyes of some, this image makes our existence seem pointless. In the eyes of others, the presence of life is seen as evidence of the amazing creative potential of nature, and the human mind is seen as a beacon in the dark, where, with consciousness, intelligence, curiosity, and love we can ponder the nature and meaning of what we see.

Some see in this a spirit in the cosmos. As Carl Sagan put it:

> "We are the local embodiment of a Cosmos grown to self-awareness… We are star-stuff pondering the stars!"

And along with prompting feelings of appreciation and wonder, the intricate order and creative potential of the natural world give a foundation for understanding why things are as they are and why things happen as they do.

Ways of the World

"In the new world view, the universe is seen
as a dynamic web of interrelated events.
None of the properties of any part of this web is fundamental;
they all follow from the properties of the other parts,
and the overall consistency of their mutual interrelations
determines the structure of the entire web."

— Fritjof Capra

The world we inhabit is vast.

Looking out, it extends beyond our planet to distant reaches of the cosmos.

Looking in is a realm as small as we can imagine, with molecules and atoms and sub-atomic particles – the basic substance of all things.

In between is a realm of non-living and living things – oceans and air, rocks and soil, and a range of plants and creatures that consume one other, metabolize and grow, then decline, decompose, and transform.

This activity appears to be guided by some general principles: that all things are composed of natural substances and act in accordance with natural laws, and that all things are dynamic and interdependent.

Rules of nature bring ordered patterns and cycles. But within this order, specific outcomes may occur due to elements of chance.

Some aspects of the modern view confound a common-sense take on what seems real, with wild leap-of-faith descriptions of the nature of time, energy, matter, and other fundamentals. Many details remain unknown, and some, perhaps, may forever be unknowable. But these details are not needed to accept a general view – that natural processes are the guiding force in all that is.

It's well beyond the scope of this book to attempt to describe what's known about modern physics, cosmology, chemistry, and other sciences. Instead, we'll highlight some general principles that inform a naturalist worldview and can contribute to spiritual responses.

General principles

All things are composed of natural substances

All that exists in the cosmos took form as aftereffects of the Big Bang. Expanding energy formed as particles, and particles formed as atoms. And with substances and forces acting in accordance with their natures, galaxies, stars, and planets took form.

On Earth, most substance consists of matter that spun off from the Sun. Also, most energy on Earth comes from the Sun. Atoms combined as molecules, forming rocks and water and air. In time, some types of molecules combined into organic forms and became parts of living things.

Much in this can easily be envisioned in natural terms. The motion of planets can be seen as due to principles of physics; and, in the patterns in crystals and snowflakes, heat from a fire, and the light prism displayed as a rainbow we can appreciate the order in nature.

Living things, though, give a sense of something different. Some natural aspects are acknowledged, as in the need for oxygen and water in cells. We appreciate how drugs can relieve pain and that living bodies require nutrients and how after death (dust to dust) physical bodies decompose and their substance becomes parts of other things. But, beyond this, some things seem more than wholly physical. For example, it's hard to envision how thoughts and feelings occur as a product of the activity of cells. These are important questions and will be examined in other sections of this book. But, while the processes in these phenomena are not yet fully understood, nothing beyond the natural world seems able to explain them.

A factor that can be considered is the principle of "emergence," which describes how some combinations result in entities that are fundamentally different than the sum of their parts. (This has been described as "something else from nothing but.") For example:

Water has qualities that are not present in hydrogen or oxygen.

A living cell has qualities that are not present in molecular interactions.

A human being is able to act in ways that are different from those of its cells.

Emergence can be seen in the self-formation of sand dunes, cities, and online social networks; and it is central to naturalist ways of understanding how the cosmos and life on Earth came to be. In contrast to a top-down view that all was created by a designer (God), emergence offers a bottom-up explanation for how complexity can arise from simpler forms, where natural entities – each acting in accordance with its nature – interact in ways that result in novel entities and capabilities.

At each level of complexity, an atom still acts as an atom, a molecule still acts as a molecule, and a cell still acts as a cell. But, when these interact in particular configurations, novel qualities may emerge that are not able to be understood by examining just the nature of the parts. As Loyal Rue put it, "Emergence is about new realities, but that does not mean that some new kind of stuff enters the picture. What enters the picture is new relationships between components that are already there ... When existing parts enter into new dynamical relations, new realities appear."

All things act in accordance with natural laws

Just as what-things-are is natural substance, how and why things occur is due to natural forces and processes (which, as patterns in these are recognized, may be described as natural laws).

Many natural processes are familiar, with concepts such as gravity, force and mass, principles of waves, and molecular bonding being taught as part of high school education. With many real-life applications – in falling objects, moving cars, and the actions of billiard balls, magnets, and levers – these explain things we deal with every day.

Some other aspects of nature are more abstract, involving realms that most people never have reason to deal with. But, as scientists described atomic structure and this was confirmed with the explosion of an atomic bomb, and as other theories led to technological advances (first in electricity, x-rays, and radio waves, and more recently with internet transmission and products ranging from microwave ovens to cell phones), we find ourselves persuaded and inclined to believe that what the scientists tell us is true. And, with these types of demonstrations as evidence, we become inclined to accept other concepts that scientists explain (whether or not we're able to grasp them), in which electromagnetic forces, laws of thermodynamics, relativity, and quantum theory can be accepted as explaining aspects of our world.

Beyond a point, as proposals become increasingly abstract, questions emerge and a skepticism may exist – as concepts such as anti-matter and multiple histories stretch the limits of imagination and credulity. Here, as has always occurred, the bounds of what seems "known" meet the realm of things not yet well understood. Beyond this lies a realm of mystery – an acknowledgment that much remains unknown. Some of these new ideas can be ignored, as things that don't seem to matter much in our lives. But, along with this, based on available knowledge (and a sense of what seems possible or plausible), we each make our own best estimation about what we *believe*.

All things are dynamic and interdependent

Basic substances are constant and universal. A carbon atom is the same in an elephant, a human, or a piece of coal. Hydrogen atoms in our water may have been spinning, without change, since the time the Earth was formed. But, while some substances (such as quartz) remain stable for millions of years, many things break apart and reconfigure.

Nothing is lost or destroyed. Mass/energy is transferred. Substance becomes part of other forms. In this dynamic world, change and transformation are the rule, and most objects are fleeting incarnations.

Fritjof Capra drew parallels between modern physics and Eastern religion. For example, in observing that "the force of electric attraction between the positively charged atomic nucleus and the negatively charged electrons ... is the basis of all solids, liquids, and gases, and also of all living organisms," he recognized a connection with the concept of yin/yang, where apparent opposites such as active/passive, male/female, good/evil, etc. represent aspects of the same reality, and that each may be required for the other to be and act as it does.

Capra pointed to a dynamic cosmos in which, at all levels – from sub-atomic particles to the activities of living beings on Earth to the galaxies and stars in the cosmos – all is in motion and constantly changing. This motion is an essential part of all that is. Time is, basically, motion. Heat, also, is motion. As Capra put it, "the activity of matter is the very essence of its being ... The whole universe is thus engaged in endless motion and activity; in a continual cosmic dance of energy."

A related point is the interrelations among all things. This applies on the level of physics and chemistry. It also applies to ecosystems, where each entity affects others and is unable to exist without the whole.

Randomness and chance

As systems act in ways that reflect a natural order, some aspects may include elements of chance. Examples of this can be seen every day – in the toss of a coin or a hand of cards to someone winning the daily lottery, or in near misses and tragic accidents in cars. A tree falls, and someone is trapped beneath it and killed, while the person right next to them is unharmed.

Central aspects of our lives occur due to chance. One sperm, among millions, fertilized an egg. Then, based on the mix of genes, we became a boy or a girl, taller or shorter, with particular color in our hair and eyes, and with distinctive talents, types of intelligence, and susceptibilities to diseases. Had the genes arranged in different ways, a different child would have been born. A chance meeting can lead to a job. I met my wife when she stood next to me in a crowd.

Being inclined to look for patterns, we may ask "Why?" (or "Why me?" or "Why did it happen just like this?"). We may wonder if things happened "for a reason."

A reason always exists. But this often relates more to groups than individuals.

Hundreds of pogies swim ahead of bluefish chasing a meal. A fisherman casts a trolling hook, which snags one of the pogies. Then a bluefish chomps down, and the fisherman reels it in. Why this particular pogie? Why this particular bluefish, but not others?

The reason is – no reason, or no reason that could have been known or avoided. Chances were good that a pogie and a bluefish would be caught. But, had the fisherman cast a bit sooner, or a bit stronger or more to the left, a different pogie would have been snagged and a different bluefish would have been caught.

Scientists look at random events in different ways.

One view is that all is determined. So, as an object in motion has a trajectory and force, a grand chain of events occurs as it encounters other objects, with A causing B, and B leading to C, and on and on ... In this view, all, in theory, could be predicted, if we had sufficient knowledge of the moving parts. The catch, of course, is that we don't have sufficient knowledge. So, as we look at weather, we recognize outcomes as due to atmospheric forces but, due to many complex interactions, it is impossible to predict 100% accurately or more than a few days out. Here, all is seen as occurring due to potentially knowable forces, and our limited ability to predict is not seen as involving "chance," but due to our limited understanding of the moving parts.

An alternative view is that some things are not, inherently, predictable. This includes perspectives of quantum physics where, within highly ordered systems, the action of the smallest particles of matter cannot be known. Another factor is living creatures acting in ways that others, and they themselves, cannot predict.

Reflections

As it considers cosmic forces at the core of all that is, a naturalist view can be seen as impersonal and cold. But, as it can include a sense of a world of wonders and a world with mystery and illusion, it can also prompt emotional responses.

A world of wonders

A naturalist view shows a world of impressive order, with massive power and scope, infinite space and time, and intricate actions and interrelation. This can be recognized as magnificent and beautiful, and worthy of appreciation and reverence. And, as the conditions that enable our lives, this can be seen as being of ultimate importance.

The ongoing quest of science works to understand more. And, as pieces are revealed, we find additional marvels to behold.

A world of illusion

Much of what exists is not as it appears to us to be.

One part of this is related to the limits of our sensory perceptions. We can't hear a dog whistle and, without special tools, we can't see infrared light or the world of microscopic objects.

Many things are more or different than they appear. For example, a rock appears to be a solid object. Yet we now understand that, beyond what we feel with our fingers and see with our eyes, the object is not, in fact, motionless and solid. Instead, it is an amalgam of activity, with electrons orbiting atomic nuclei at high-speeds. Further, the rock is not solid. Great spaces exist between the nuclei and electron clouds. So what seems still is in motion. What seems solid is, for the most part, empty space.

Beyond this, the matter in a particle is a function of its energy (as in Einstein's $E = mc^2$), and energy, itself, is a dynamic quantity associated with activity or processes. As quantum theory and other aspect of modern physics are revealing, much of what exists is very different than how it appears, and several perspectives on "reality" are available.

For practical purposes, most things act in ways that fit with how they seem. And, despite limits in our abilities to perceive and understand, an everyday sense of how things are works well for most of what we need. But, as scientists are beginning to grasp, and consistent with the Eastern concept of Maya, the world is different in many ways than it appears to be, and much of what we perceive can be said to be illusion.

A world with mystery

Beyond acknowledging illusion, and despite all attempts to understand, some important things are not yet well understood. These include fundamental aspects of nature – matter, energy, and time – and non-material things like consciousness and thought.

The lack of clear and convincing explanations for fundamental things supports the arguments of those who point to limits in science. The sense here is that, since a naturalist view, like belief in God, includes unanswered questions, the beliefs and theories of either may be valid. An important difference, though, is that rather than defending an ancient image of how things are, the whole focus in science is to understand, with a willingness to reshape views to match what comes to be known.

A naturalist perspective acknowledges that some questions may not have answers that we are able to comprehend. It recognizes that some views now held may eventually be revised, and that each time new insights are gained, new realms of unanswered questions will arise.

With this, a realm of mystery exists beyond what is able to be known. Rather than viewing this as a limit or weakness, many embrace mystery as humble and realistic. (Imagine – mere humans being able to decipher and grasp the forces that guide the cosmos?) And as we recognize feelings of wonder and awe, some experience something like the reverence that others frame as the unknowable nature of God.

Life

"If you put effort into understanding what life is,
you will feel wonder."

— Paul Fleischman

With a view that it occurs due to wholly natural processes, life is partly mysterious and partly well-understood.

The parts that are understood have led to "miraculous" advances in medicine, with prevention and cure of diseases, *in vitro* fertilization, organ transplantation, and many other techniques that let us live longer and healthier lives.

The parts that are not understood prompt questions – like how collections of cells can produce thoughts, feelings, and desires; and, if no intangible soul controls our bodies, what sort of creature are we, and why do we do the things we do?

The known and unknown can also prompt emotional responses, with a sense of wonder at the birth of a child and a sense of amazement at the beautiful and varied forms of life that have evolved over billions of years.

Since life ("being itself") is the foundation of what we are, it seems worthwhile to try to understand what we can.

What is life?

No single description gives a full sense of what it means to be alive.

One view looks at life as self-sustaining chemical systems. All living things are composed of a handful of substances (carbohydrates, fats, proteins, nucleic acids, water, salts, and adenosine phosphates). These are all products, mainly, of a small number of atoms (carbon, hydrogen, nitrogen, oxygen, phosphorus, and sulfur) and provide energy and raw materials for construction and maintenance of cells.

Another perspective on life is purposeful activity, where, unlike rocks, each living thing takes actions to enable it (or its species) to survive and thrive and reproduce. This occurs in amoebae, plants, and worms, as well as reptiles, mammals, and humans – as each approaches food and optimal temperatures and mates, and avoids things that cause harm.

Each living thing is an individual – a "self" – that interacts with its environment.

Origin and evolution of life

The exact steps that occurred in the origin of life are not well understood, but a general process is thought to have occurred. In this, substances known to be present in the early environment of Earth took form, through chemical reactions, as molecules that interacted in ways that enabled cell formation. A critical step was assembly of nucleotides (similar to RNA), which had the ability to reproduce themselves.

One view is that, when lipids combined in ways that enclosed a nucleotide and water, the first type of proto-cell had taken form.

This had an inside and an outside, and functioned in ways that were separate from the rest of the environment.

Over time, as these cells reproduced, some mutated in ways that enabled them to draw in energy-rich substances and manufacture other substances to maintain the structure and functions of the cells.

For more than 2 billion years, single-celled organisms were the only forms of life. Among these were cyanobacteria, which combined carbon dioxide, water, and energy from the Sun to produce oxygen. Over time this occurred on a massive scale, to the point of altering Earth's atmosphere in ways that enabled oxygen-dependent life.

About 500 million years ago, mutations in early cells resulted in multicellular beings. In these beings, cells were no longer independent, but performed distinctive functions in coordination with other types of cells. Further mutations led to more complex and varied creatures – as hearts and lungs and brains emerged, and as fish evolved to amphibians, reptiles, birds, and mammals.

Due to common ancestry, many creatures have similar steps in fetal development and similar body structures and organs. As brains became increasingly complex, each retained some structures and ways of processing from creatures that came earlier in evolution. Due to this, many aspects of our needs and behaviors trace back to early forms of life, and some are shared with those in other creatures.

Nature of life

Some general processes and principles can be seen as aspects of life.

Life involves activity

Cells are constantly active, with intake and outflow of molecules as structures are assembled, damaged parts are repaired, and waste products are released. Activity is constant in multicellular systems, with respiration, digestion, production of hormones, and circulation of blood occurring in all animals. Each being is active – obtaining food, mating, and interacting with other living things.

Activity requires energy

Growth and maintenance of cells requires energy, which is obtained from the metabolism of food. For a time (the duration of a life) body structures run counter to the physical principle of entropy (the natural tendency of complex structures to break apart). Then, when energy is no longer available or able to be effectively used, activity declines, then ceases, and the organism dies, and the substances it was formed from decompose and become parts of other living and non-living things.

Most energy in food traces back to the Sun. This occurs directly in cyanobacteria, algae, and plants where, through photosynthesis, carbon dioxide (from the atmosphere) and hydrogens (from water) are converted into sugars, which are used and stored for energy. It occurs indirectly in food chains, where many animals (herbivores) obtain energy by eating the plants, and other animals (carnivores) obtain the energy by eating other animals.

All living things are interdependent

The food chain shows one piece in a broader picture where, in order to exist, each species needs many other species. And, for an individual to be healthy, the group and the ecosystem need to be healthy.

Each non-photosynthetic creature needs living things that provide their food. These living things, in turn, need other substances and living things that sustain them. All rely on and nourish one another in a complex "web of life" in which particular species exist only due to the presence of other living things.

Each has a niche and exists because it is able to survive by behaving in certain ways. With this, millions of varied species, often beautiful and odd, form complex ecosystems. And, as cells exist as part of organisms, and organisms exist in groups, and groups interact with and depend on other species, a collection of life encompasses the planet. This image has been described as a "superorganism" – Gaia. If taken literally, the concept is flawed. But, as metaphor, it highlights the countless interactions and interdependencies among all living things worldwide.

As part of this interdependence, in a number of species, individuals are inseparable from groups. Many, including humans, exist in families, tribes, herds, schools, or flocks. Many, including humans, require some nurturing and teaching of the young. And for many, including humans, the strategies that enabled them to find and thrive in an eco-niche include their tendency to cooperate in groups.

Reflections

A naturalist view of life can bring a sense of connection – with other people, other creatures, and all of nature. It shows a common origin, tracing back to ancient times, with some common needs, types of awareness, and ways of behaving.

It can also prompt a sense of appreciation and wonder that such a rare and amazing thing could come to be.

As the most fundamental aspect of our being, life can be seen, at the very least, as important and special and, in the eyes of many, as sacred. And as we value life, we can also value the food, water, and ecosystems that sustain it.

The complexity of human life is hard to envision, as the trillion cells in our bodies act in close coordination to regulate heartbeat, breathing, temperature, and digestion and enable vision, hearing, memory, and thought. We marvel as newborn turtles know to move toward the sea and birds migrate for thousands of miles and fish assemble in protective clusters.

Much of this is deep-seated – genetic, automatic, not requiring reflection or choices. As we come to appreciate the extent to which innate behaviors enable many species to thrive, we can recognize in ourselves, and come to trust and respect, our own intuitive ways of responding. And as we observe cooperation, kindness, and problem-solving in elephants, dolphins, dogs, birds, and other creatures, we can appreciate that we humans are hardly alone in having intelligence, awareness, and feelings.

While the processes that enable these things are increasingly well-understood, unanswered questions remain and many suspect that something more than biology, some type of living spirit, must be involved. But since this view also has unanswered questions, we may take a naturalist view that:

> something in the nature of atoms
> includes the potential
> to combine in ways that result in life.

One way of looking at this was described by Fritjof Capra:

> "When we look at the world around us, we find that we are not thrown into chaos and randomness but are part of a great order, a grand symphony of life. Every molecule in our body was once part of previous bodies – living or nonliving – and will be a part of future bodies. In this sense, our body will not die but will live on, again and again, because life lives on. We share not only

life's molecules but also its basic principles of organization with the rest of the living world. And since our mind, too, is embodied, our concepts and metaphors are embedded in the web of life together with our bodies and brains. We belong to the universe, we are at home in it, and this experience of belonging can make our lives profoundly meaningful."

Being Human

"Know thyself"

—Inscribed at the
Temple of Apollo at Delphi

"Only wisdom
based on self-understanding …
will save us."

— E. O. WILSON

A naturalist sense of being human differs in important ways from traditional views in Western culture. In contrast to a dualist image of a physical body and an eternal soul, we see ourselves as biological beings – a particular type of primate – having much in common with other creatures, but also in many ways unique. Far more than is generally acknowledged, our choices and actions can be unconscious or automatic, and emotions and intuitions often play larger roles than rational analysis.

Within the short span of a few centuries, our population and technologies have increased to the point of destroying ecosystems and causing the extinction of thousands of species. Some are now describing this time as the start of a new era – the Anthropocene – in which the dominant force affecting the natural environments on Earth is human activity.

Will we use our intelligence to find ways to form a peaceful and sustainable world?

Or will the tribal, short-sighted, aggressive parts of ourselves prevail, and lead to social and environmental devastation?

Who are we?

What are we?

Why we do the things we do?

And how might we learn to do better?

The human animal

As we consider what we are today, we can look back through evolution – to a progression, over millions of years, from primate and prehuman ancestors to modern humans, including:

Australopithecus	3 million years ago
Homo erectus	1 million years ago
Homo sapiens	c. 150,000 years ago

Some aspects of our mental processes have roots in prehuman times and contribute to how we understand and act. But over time, a line was crossed – from capabilities and behaviors that we can recognize in primates to distinctly human types of intelligence and awareness. The earliest evidence of this can be seen in crafted hand axes and other tools, tracing back to more than a million years ago. Further advances, seen at sites from 30,000+ years ago, are revealed in cave art, musical instruments, and burials. A modern mind was clearly present by the time of Plato in ancient Greece, and advances in knowledge have led from hunter/gatherer tribal existence to agricultural, manufacturing, and modern high-tech eras and lifestyles.

Common qualities

Much in how we think and what we do is shared by people and groups in cultures around the world.

Universal Human Qualities		
Mental capabilities	**Modes of expression**	**Feelings**
Abstraction	Language	Affection
Anticipation	Joke	Ambivalence
Beliefs	Metaphor	Attachment
Classification	Myth	Emotions
Comparison	Narrative	Empathy
Distinguish	Music	Envy
Dreams	Poetry	Fears
Explanation	Proverbs	Hope
Imagery	Special speech	Pride
Intention	Symbolism	Shame
Interpretation		
Logical notions		
Meaning		
Memory		
Person (concept of)		
Plan		
Recognize		

Behaviors/Customs Present in all Cultures		
Athletic sports	Bodily adornment	Calendar
Cooking	Cooperative labor	Cosmology
Courtship	Dancing	Dream interpretation
Education	Ethics	Food taboos
Funeral rites	Games	Gestures
Gift giving	Greetings	Hair styles
Incest taboos	Inheritance rules	Joking
Language	Law	Magic
Marriage	Medicine	Penal sanctions
Personal names	Property rights	Puberty customs
Religious ritual	Sexual restrictions	Status differentiation
Superstitions	Tool making	Trade
Visiting	Weaving	

Many practices are clearly learned, but a number of inclinations and abilities appear to be innate. These include some traits all humans share, like attraction to sugars, aversion to snakes, and sexual desire. They also include some intuitions that play roles in moral judgments, such as empathy and aversion to incest. Some personal qualities also appear to be set or influenced at birth, as genetic factors not only shape our size and appearance but also contribute to aptitude for music, math, and some other abilities and aspects of personality (as in having a calm or anxious disposition). As E. O. Wilson put it, "The question of interest is no longer whether human social behavior is genetically determined; it is to what extent."

Mental processes

A naturalist view holds that perceptions and desires all originate in the body and brain. Or, to break it down further, these occur mainly due to the activity of billions of nerve cells that receive and transmit electrochemical impulses. Our thoughts and feelings are the products of biochemical activity. And while it seems to us that a self – "me" – is in our heads, looking out through eyes, reading this book, and making choices, there is no evidence that an intangible spirit or soul animates our bodies, meaning that "free will" is different and less free than is widely assumed.

Parts of this view fit easily with what we understand. We know that brain damage from strokes and tumors can affect cognition and moods. Some drugs and types of trauma can increase aggression. Changes in the brain can cause changes in the person. And when the brain stops, the person no longer exists.

But, beyond this general concept, a mystery remains – in *how* activity in brain cells becomes what we think and feel.

A number of pieces are beginning to be understood. For example, Antonio Damasio and others have shown that much of what we "feel" when we are anxious, irritable, or euphoric involves changes in heart rate, breathing, and release of endorphins and other chemicals. And when considering complex mental states, such as consciousness, current scientific views focus more on interactions among cognitive systems (including memory, language, and attention) than on activity at the level of nerve cells.

Research has also shown that, in contrast to historical views of humans as largely rational; unconscious, emotional, and intuitive processes are increasingly recognized as playing important roles. Jonathan Haidt described a number of examples of how intuitive perceptions (or "gut reactions") can shape our views of what is right or wrong. Using an analogy of a rider on an elephant, where the rider believes he is in control, but it is actually the elephant that sets the direction, he said:

> "Automatic processes run the human mind, just as they have been running animal minds for 500 million years, so they're

very good at what they do, like software that has been improved through thousands of product cycles. When human beings evolved the capacity for language and reasoning at some point in the last million years, the brain did not rewire itself to hand over the reins to a new and inexperienced charioteer. Rather, the rider (language-based reasoning) evolved because it did something useful for the elephant."

In Haidt's view, part of what the rational brain contributes is creating plausible explanations for why we acted in ways that were mainly intuitive.

Intuitive thinking evolved and persists because it has proven effective. But intuitive approaches don't always match what is accurate. This accounts for common misperceptions (like fear of airplane crashes, where risk is greater when travelling by car) and for superstitions and optical illusions. It accounts for how, as we consider what to do, we may at times be of "two minds" as intuitive and rational mental processes lead to different conclusions. Also, in a mental tendency that has doubtless contributed to survival, we pay more attention to bad news, risks, and problems than to the good things in our lives (which is why reminders and techniques for shifting focus, as encouraged by psychologists and religions, may be needed to help us notice things that we have reason to be grateful for).

Reflections

As we consider why we do what we do and how to become our better selves, naturalists begin with what can be known of human nature. Part of this involves learning to recognize and when to trust "gut feelings." Part also involves an honest look in the mirror. And as this shows intuitive tendencies that may, at times, contribute to problems, it can also point to inclinations that can contribute to responses.

So, for example, if it can be recognized that avoidance or fear of "others" is common and innate, then finding ways to prompt empathy, kindness, and other positive intuitive responses can be encouraged as a counterbalance. As in addressing drug addiction, if the rational brain is not responsible for choices that are made, limited benefit can come from strategies directed at the rational. In considering these and other challenges, a goal is to better understand factors that shape behavior, and to make use of what is known, rather than aspiring to unachievable ideals.

Intuitive views are also thought to play roles in some aspects of religious beliefs, as in feeling that things happen for a reason, and there is a purpose for our existence, and that whatever guides the cosmos may have awareness and intent.

Even self-described atheists can show these patterns of thinking, where, despite not believing in a God that may intervene in events, they may at times speak out loud to plead for an outcome (as they call "Go!" as they watch a hit baseball that they hope will clear the fence, or yell "No!" as they curse the fates when things go wrong). A study showed that, despite stating that they rejected supernatural explanations, when they were asked why they thought that major events in their lives had occurred, a majority of atheists answered that these were "meant to be" or happened "because they needed to learn a lesson."

We can, and often do, override these mental tendencies. But, because gut feelings come easily and may be strong, it can require both knowledge and effort to override them.

Many people have had moments when they felt a sense of timelessness, oneness, peace, love, or illumination. A Pew survey reported that almost 50% of respondents said they have had a religious or mystical experience, defined as a "moment of sudden religious insight or awakening." In traditional religions, these may be understood as feeling the presence of God. From a naturalist perspective, these are seen as patterns of activity in the brain.

An area of study, sometimes called neurotheology, is examining what occurs with these types of perceptions, and also in meditation and prayer. This research has confirmed the age-old recognition that these states may be induced by certain drugs, disease, sensory deprivation, and fever. Art, at times, can lead to spiritual feelings, with patterns of light and sound, harmony and rhythm, repetition and variation.

Although research is in the early stages, some studies have given clues about the processes involved. For example, some studies of meditation have shown decreased activity in an area of the brain that plays roles in distinguishing the self from objects in the world. This, in turn, may contribute to a sense of oneness that can occur during meditation. Activities such as chanting, repetitive prayer, and repetition of a mantra can disengage parts of the usual waking mind. This can lead to relaxation, with a sense of peace or calm; and it may alter aspects of attention and thought in ways that enable the mind to shift focus toward ideals.

One part of being human includes the potential for spiritual perceptions. Many people never experience such a thing and may be skeptical of what others describe. For some others, these types of experiences can be deeply moving and unforgettable, and they can produce a desire to understand or repeat them.

Being Religious

"Why bother about spirituality?
Well, why bother about love or beauty?
It is part of the richest flavor of life."

— JEROME A. STONE

An ancient burial site shows a body adorned with ochre and beads. The positioning shows signs of respect, and the presence of hunting tools suggests the idea of an afterlife. This type of response to death is one of the earliest signs of something we now see as religious.

Whether we think of ourselves as religious or not, most people, at times, consider religious questions. We may also experience religious feelings. This can be as simple as responding to beauty, order, and unanswered questions about the world, which may prompt appreciation and wonder. It may also, on occasion, give a sense of something more – in feeling part of all that is, with a sense of clarity and meaning in what we see.

As we acknowledge these types of perceptions, and as we recognize some things (like the life of a child) as being important or "sacred," and as we try to act in accordance with our beliefs, we can each be seen as having our own spiritual sense or religious orientation.

As something that has been present in all cultures and times, religion can be seen as part of human nature. And as a way of responding to questions or concerns that have no simple answers, religion can be seen, like art, as a way of exploring or expressing insights that may require more than words.

As is shown in the collection of quotes in the Appendix, being religious has many dimensions. It also tends to include some common themes: morality and values, personal growth or transformation, and a sense of something transcendent (where, along with and as part of what we are able to touch or see, is a sense of something more timeless and universal).

It involves attitudes, feelings, and actions related to values and beliefs.

A religious orientation can bind groups together with common practices. It can be valuable to individuals, as it provides a framework for considering spiritual questions. It can also be uplifting, in offering, in the words of William James, "a meaning, or an enchantment and glory to the common objects of life" and "a feeling that great and wondrous things are in the air."

Being a religious naturalist

When the idea of being religious is considered with respect to naturalist views, it tends not to include some of what first comes to mind when people think of religion.

It doesn't involve devotion to a deity.
Instead, it looks to nature, and responds to appreciation of the natural world.

It doesn't mean being a member of an established religious group.
Instead, it can be largely a personal orientation.

But, as was discussed on a previous page, it does include active interest in spiritual questions. And, as Jerome Stone described, it can include a view that "there are religious aspects of this world which can be appreciated within a naturalist framework."

One perspective on what it can mean to be religious was described by Loyal Rue. This begins with a view of religion in which a central mythic story is shared by a group. This includes cosmological ideas – about how things are in the world; and moral ideas – about which things matter, and what is right and good.

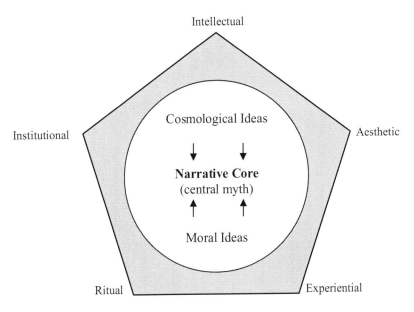

Several strategies support the central myth. Some of these are intellectual, as in books or discussions that present the story and interpret or debate its relevance to our lives. Some involve aesthetic (artistic) depictions or ritual responses, or ways of encouraging and understanding religious experiences. Institutions form, with teachers and leaders, as groups consider and respond to the story.

As was described in the chapter on Origins, for most naturalists, the central myth begins with the scientific story of the Big Bang and evolution. And beyond this description of how we came to be, additional stories can expand the mythic core, framing what we might wish for and work toward as an ideal world, and challenges that may be faced along the way.

> One image of a world that we might aspire to was shown by Thomas Berry, who described a potential future "Ecozoic Era" where humans live in balance with other creatures and natural environments in ways that will be long-term sustainable.

> Part of the challenge was discussed by E. O. Wilson, who looked at humans as advanced primates that, after thousands of years as hunter/gatherers, grew too fast with no plan into a crowded modern world, where the lives we live are not the lives our brains evolved to.

Rue distinguished a *religious* naturalist from a nonreligious naturalist by saying that a religious naturalist "takes nature to heart." By this he meant caring – about the whole of the natural world, including people (near and far) and other creatures, ecosystems, and all that enables us to be.

With this, one part of being religious, as a naturalist, has to do with acknowledging, appreciating, and trying to understand and act on feelings that have long been seen as spiritual or religious. This can include the sense of wonder that may be felt at the birth of a child, the deep emotions that accompany a death, and the sense of mystery that comes with unanswerable questions. It can include a sense of awe at the beauty in nature, and what Ursula Goodenough described as "the gratitude and astonishment of being alive."

It can also include appreciation of some practices that have long been important in traditional religions, and of wisdom that can be found in stories, poems, and prayers from a range of religious and cultural traditions.

Reflections

Religion has been present in all cultures and times because it serves important roles. It provides standards for moral behavior, reasons for hope, and a framework for considering important questions. Although it is a realm of ideals, its strength and staying power are practical.

William James discussed how religion is not about beliefs, but about life, where "a larger, richer, more satisfying life is, in the last analysis, the end of religion. The love of life, at any and every level of development, is the religious impulse."

People vary in the extent to which they are attracted to religion or spirituality. Interest can also vary at points in life, and may become more active as young adults reconsider what they were taught as children; in responses to illness, loss, or major changes; or in relation to direct experiences, where we may be moved by perceptions of *something* that seems important, intriguing, beautiful, and true.

With an understanding of religion as an attitude toward life, it's hard to see how, at least occasionally, some type of spiritual/religious sense would not be acknowledged. Albert Einstein referred to something like this where, as he made it clear that he did not believe in an active personal God (or in an afterlife or supernatural miracles), he recognized and celebrated a sense of mystery.

"He who knows it not and can no longer wonder, no longer feel amazement, is as good as dead, a snuffed-out candle."

Alongside this, he felt a deep appreciation that he saw no better way of describing than religious. In one of several attempts to explain this, he said:

> "It was the experience of mystery – even if mixed with fear – that engendered religion. A knowledge of the existence of something we cannot penetrate, of the manifestations of the profoundest reason and the most radiant beauty, which are only accessible to our reason in their most elementary forms – it is this knowledge and this emotion that constitute the truly religious attitude; in this sense, and in this alone, I am a deeply religious man."

Something like this can be felt by those who have a naturalist worldview; where whatever in us may, at times, have a sense of something spiritual or religious is understood in relation to what we can see in looking to nature.

Ways of exploring, appreciating, and acting on this are the focus of the rest of this book.

Part 2:
Practices

"So now we can talk practices.
And we can call them religious practices …
because they make us pause and consider.
And if we do them with awareness,
they orient us to our common best interest,
which is to live in balance with each other and the world."

— Ron Phares

Beyond seeing how we *can* look to nature as a focus of attention, what types of things might we *do* – to act in ways that reflect what we aspire to and believe?

For some, the answer is simple, where spiritual practices are things we're doing already.

Beyond these, a wide range of activities can be considered. Some may be based on responses to nature; others can be adopted or adapted from traditional religions. Some may be done frequently; others may be done occasionally or rarely. Some are done individually; others may be done in groups.

This range of options is similar to Hinduism, where people are encouraged to seek paths that suit their personal temperament.

And, with parallels to aspects of Japanese Shinto tradition, no weekly services are offered, no observance is required, and each person can decide what (if anything) to do, and when; as they may perform rituals or other activities in their homes, or visit a temple when they choose. (For many naturalists, the "temple" is outdoors, or in music venues, libraries, or museums.)

As will be discussed on the following pages, practices may be done to orient the mind – toward spiritual and healthy attitudes, or to engage in a path toward self-improvement or transformation.

Some other practices go beyond activities that may be good for us, ourselves, and may be done to help others and contribute to our communities (and, perhaps also, to the world as a whole) to try to put our values into practice.

A common theme in many practices is that they can bring a sense of connection.

Practices That
Orient the Mind

"These experiences lift us up out of our narrow selves
and give us a glimpse – if only temporary –
of another way to view things."

— ELLEN IDLER

A number of practices can shift attention away from concerns of daily life and toward more spiritual perspectives. These can remind us of what we see as important or ideal. And they can bring periods of what has been described as "sacred time", where much like entering a cathedral can give a sense of something holy, entering a pine grove, meditating, or losing ourselves in music can bring a sense of this being a special time – where, for a while, we may feel surrounded by what seems beautiful and good, and connected, calm, or attentive to things that we might not otherwise have noticed.

These types of activities can be enjoyable and useful when they occur, as they shift our gaze and help us to see with different eyes. They may also contribute longer-term (as is discussed in the next section) to spiritual growth or transformation.

A number of general approaches may be used, including:

Encounters with nature

Encounters with art

Meditation

Prayer

Rituals

Pilgrimages and retreats

Encounters with nature

Gerald May described "the power of the slowing," where nature can slow us down to its pace. For example, the sound of waves can lead to a meditative state.

E. O. Wilson feels that part of the appeal is based in evolution; where, being descended from ancestors who, for millennia, lived mostly outdoors, we can feel at home, with a pleasant sense of something right and good in natural settings. (Wilson described this as "biophilia.") Some feel that the modern absence of natural environments can cause psychic disorientation, which has been described as "nature deficit disorder."

Beyond affecting our pace or mood, a walk in the woods or by the shore, or watching a sunset, observing birds, and many other activities can teach or remind us about the ways of the natural world, and reacquaint us with ways of being that are broader and more ancient and enduring than our own personal and social concerns. And, beyond what may occur when we're in natural settings, spiritual perceptions can occur in response to bits of nature in our homes, like flowers in a vase on the kitchen table.

Michael Barrett discussed how "a scientifically informed mindfulness" is something that fits well with a religious naturalist orientation. One approach to this is described in Chet Raymo's book, *The Path*, where he discussed how, along with enjoying the walk he took to work each day – on a path through woods and a field and across a stream – he took time to learn about the plants and birds and animals and bugs that lived in this ecosystem, and also some of the history of the place (where some of the landscape had been shaped by an ancient glacier, and how a dam and stone walls came to be). With this, over time, as he noticed details, he could also see how these were parts of the whole, and how he was also part of this local ecosystem.

A related activity can come with the Swedish idea of smultronstället, which means "the place of the wild strawberries." It refers to a place that can bring a certain mood, that you discovered and now feel is your own. Mike Comins, in *A Wild Faith*, describes the impact of these places – how, by observing the local creatures and plants, and by returning in different seasons and in different weather and times of day, we can come in time to know one place well, and with this get a richer sense of wider nature; and how, in gazing at the surroundings or listening with no thoughts, a sense of calm, like meditation, may come in.

Encounters with art

Some have described music or art as "my religion" – as, at times, these can cause us to "lose ourselves" or feel at one with others or have a sense that we've experienced something meaningful. As Gabrielle Roth put it, "We dance ... to disappear in something bigger ... to fall in love with the spirit in all things."

Spiritual feelings can occur when creating art, in responding to art, or joining in to sing along. They can be sought – through attending performances or visiting gardens, museums, or other liminal places – and they can be appreciated at random moments, prompted by art we stop to notice in the course of a day.

As they can give ways of understanding that speak more to feelings than thoughts, music, theater, poetry, photography, painting, dance, stories, and collage can each stimulate, soothe, intrigue, and reveal in their own particular ways.

Other practices

Meditation and prayer are valuable parts of a number of religious traditions.

Meditation can calm the mind and slow the body down. When done occasionally, it can give a relaxing change of pace. When done regularly and long-term, it can be a way of training the mind – to shift from destructive habits toward a state of greater enlightenment and peace. Many approaches are available, including those from Christian as well as Eastern traditions, and including techniques that involve walking, as well as sitting. Some approaches can be learned quickly and require only small amounts of time. For example, one description of mindful meditation, as taught by Thich Nhat Hanh, says:

> "just become aware of your breath, and through that come into the present moment ... If you are mindful, or fully present in the here and now, anxiety disappears and a sense of timelessness takes hold, allowing our highest qualities of kindness and compassion to emerge."

Transcendental meditation involves repetition of a mantra (a simple, often meaningless, word). This has been shown in medical studies to reduce heart rate and breathing and produce changes in hormones and responses to stress, and distinctive patterns of brain activity. A goal of this technique has been described as a state of inner calmness, and a Westernized version, taught in medical schools, has been described as "the relaxation response."

Some other techniques may be done to reduce "chatter" in our heads or decrease focus on self/ego, and can lead to a feeling of greater connection with all around us.

Prayer can be a form of introspection (and, can be useful even for those who have no belief that a deity is listening). Much like writing in a journal, by diving deep and speaking honestly about hopes, gratitude, and fears, the act of considering things that matter and expressing what we feel can be a way of inviting and (sometimes) gaining insight.

Rituals may be performed to mark life events and remind ourselves of important stories or ideas. They can also be ways of responding to events or mysteries that we cannot fathom, and that can't be dealt with rationally.

Some rituals can be adaptations of what is done in established religions. Words may be spoken before meals to show gratitude for food. And, in gatherings with family and friends at weddings, funerals, or other occasions, wording and actions may be adapted to reflect themes in a naturalist orientation, instead of a focus on God or other aspects of religious traditions.

Likewise, some holidays may be reinterpreted, where the Christmas/New Year "holiday season" may focus on the winter solstice, and the return of Spring may be marked alongside Easter, Purim, and other observances. Some naturalists observe Earth Day, birthdays of Charles Darwin or John Muir, or mark dates when ecologic or social justice laws were passed or when important gatherings occurred. Some perform rituals associated with celestial events – related to sunrise, sunset, solstices, equinoxes, or full moons. Some have naturalist-oriented ways of responding to ritual themes; for example, in choosing "natural burial", where remains might be put beneath flowers or trees so that body substance will be taken in through roots and become part of living things that might later be visited.

Some rituals have been recently created; where, as the story of escape from Egypt is told at Passover each year and stories about Jesus are told at Christmas and Easter, some naturalists participate in a ritual re-telling of the story of evolution. One version of this is the Cosmic Walk, where a spiral path is put in a large outdoor space or room, and participants start at the center and (often with candle light and music) slowly walk out, and stop at markers along the way – to reflect on steps that occurred from the Big Bang to the formation of matter, galaxies, and solar systems, and the emergence and evolution of life on Earth. Michael Dowd and Connie Barlow have done activities with children to assemble necklaces with beads that show aspects of the Big Story of the cosmos.

Some perform rituals that give reminders of important aspects of the natural world, as in Donald Crosby's suggestion that, before drinking a glass of water, we might stop and reflect on its central importance to our existence; or in ceremonial first plantings in a garden in Spring.

Some naturalists go on pilgrimages – with a journey to and physical presence in a place where important things occurred. With a spirit similar to those who visit Jerusalem, Mecca, or Mount Kailash in Tibet, some may journey to sites where naturalist ideals were realized or inspired (such as the Galapagos Islands, Yosemite, and Walden Pond), or sites closer to home that have personal meaning – to pay tribute and deepen understanding.

Some go on formal or informal retreats, which give time apart from the settings and routines of daily life; and replace these, for a time, with an environment, pace, and activities designed to contribute to spiritual orientation.

Spiritual Growth
or Transformation

> "Spiritual practice is a process of spiritual transformation.
> That is, the transformation of our essential nature."
>
> — DANIEL STRAIN

Some approaches to being religious include a goal of personal change – to come to think and act in ways that will make us better people (or to avoid destructive behaviors, or to become more at peace with ourselves). For those who are already living in relatively healthy, moral, and satisfying ways, activity may be described as "growth," with increased focus on ideals. But, for those who are suffering, troubled, regretful, or confused, activity may point toward more substantial change, which may be described as "transformation." As Patrick McNamara described this, "To let go of unworthy attachments, the old Self has to 'die,' sacrifice its old loves. Unless the old Self dies, the new Self cannot emerge or be born."

As has long been recognized by religious traditions, substantial growth involves more than good intentions and occasional activities. It can require ongoing attention and approaches that may involve bodies as well as minds, emotions as well as intellect, and formation of habits where, through repeated practice, things that once required conscious effort become automatic.

Spiritual growth can include development of religious attitudes and morality. And it can involve ongoing learning – to try to better understand how things are and why things happen as they do (in the natural world, in our social circles, and in ourselves) and to grow in the ability to make wise choices.

Developing religious attitudes

> "… religion means much more than a state of mind
> or [an] ecstatic or mystical mood.
> It's a commitment over a lifetime
> to what a person considers to be good."
>
> — JOHN HAUGHT

When Loyal Rue described how a religious naturalist "takes nature to heart," he meant an attitude of actively caring about the natural world, people, and other creatures. Spiritual practice can include keeping this and some other positive attitudes in mind, and trying to act in ways that reflect them.

This can start with a general attitude – of simply trying to be a good person. It can also involve some particular attitudes. For example:

appreciation (or gratitude),
> for being alive, and for the many good things we have;

humility,
> where we can see ourselves as small in the grand scheme of all that is, and that there's much that we're unable to understand; and

mindfulness,
in paying attention in ways that help us to see what is around us.

A number of other attitudes are widely valued, such as compassion, hope, and wonder (and also, for many, reverence). Each person can emphasize or prioritize among attitudes that can shape how we think and what we do.

Efforts to nurture these and other attitudes can involve learning – as may occur in listening to sermons and reading books about virtues and stories of admirable people and deeds. It can also involve reminders, repetition, or ritual acts that help ideas to register more strongly. As Karen Armstrong put it,

"Compassion is a practically acquired knowledge, like dancing. You must do it and practice diligently day by day."

Some express gratitude with words of thankfulness before a meal. Some get reminders of humility by gazing at the night sky.

Seeking knowledge and wisdom

"The further the spiritual evolution of mankind advances,
the more certain it seems to me
that the path to genuine religiosity does not lie through
the fear of life, and the fear of death, and blind faith,
but through striving after rational knowledge."

— ALBERT EINSTEIN

With a view that all occurs due to natural forces, it can be spiritually as well as practically useful to understand, as best we can, the nature of the natural world and why things happen as they do. As was introduced in Part 1 of this book, a huge range of topics can be explored.

In contrast to some who have voiced concern about "unweaving the rainbow" (where scientific knowledge might diminish a sense of wonder), religious naturalists tend to feel that the opposite is true – that appreciation can be enhanced by knowing more. And, beyond the awe that can come as understanding expands, increasing knowledge has provided advances in medicine more dramatic than "miracles" that once prompted belief. It can have psychic benefits, by leading to views that can help to minimize disappointments that arise from misconceptions, and by showing attitudes that can contribute to peace of mind. Knowledge can also contribute to wisdom when we're faced with moral choices or dilemmas, as it grounds decisions in how things are (as supported by evidence), rather than on views of how we think things *should* be.

As it helps us to maximize good and minimize problems, seeking knowledge can be seen as a path toward salvation (as in the root word "salve" – to alleviate suffering, soothe, or heal). And, as part of the Buddhist eight-fold path, "right understanding" can contribute to avoidance of suffering.

Different people are drawn to different topics and methods of study.

Some are mainly interested in science (or the related fields of psychology, sociology, anthropology, and history).
Others prefer the types of insights that can be gained via literature, poetry, and myth.

Some are generalists and learn a bit about many things.
Others specialize in particular areas and dive deep.

Some take and file notes and may summarize what they learn.
Others form general impressions, without much concern about details.

Some learn mainly from books, nature films, web searches, and other media.
Others prefer direct experience – in contact with people and natural settings.

Some are independent and chart their own paths.
Others follow the lead of teachers or role models.

Seeking knowledge can be done in a wholly secular way. But, as it is in the study of scripture, jnana yoga, and some other traditions, seeking knowledge can be embraced as a religious practice – a path of ongoing growth.

As some study the Bible or ponder the will of God, religious naturalists may try to understand aspects of the natural world. This can bring a sense of connection – to other people, other creatures, and the world of which we are all part. And, as increasing knowledge brings deeper layers of the picture into focus, new questions emerge and a sense of mystery remains.

Community

"People deeply need membership in a group"

— E. O. WILSON

"It's just so validating to know
that we're not alone in this way…"

A response to finding a naturalist group

While many are happy to look to nature mainly as a personal orientation, some also want to be part of a religious community.

No naturalist meeting-houses stand in prominent locations in towns. Instead, the main current options are online communities, naturalist involvement in churches or temples, and spiritual involvement in non-religious groups.

Online communities

Several groups have formed that can provide aspects of community for those who look to nature. As members live in varied locations, most interaction is online.

Most groups have websites that provide information on a range of topics, with links to books, essays, videos and events that may be of interest. Membership is largely from the United States, but also includes people in Europe, Australia, and many other parts of the world.

Some groups also have active online discussions, where people can ask questions or share thoughts on whatever topics may be of interest, and receive comments from a variety of perspectives. Many enjoy this as a role that is more active than that of parishioners in pews. They enjoy how, as ideas are traded back and forth in conversations over time, they can come to know some virtual partners well. Some participate regularly, some may comment occasionally, and others mainly listen in; and online conversations can lead to in-person gatherings.

Naturalist involvement in established churches or temples

A number of naturalists are occasional or active members of churches or temples, where in congregations that are comfortable with non-literal interpretations (or, if they choose to remain quiet or low-key about their beliefs), they can appreciate ideals and mythic value in age-old stories, and enjoy the traditions and social connections of being part of an in-person group. Some teach Sunday School, sing in the choir, or help to organize church suppers or other activities. And while they may sometimes be seen as a bit of a heretic (or may choose to embrace that role), in a number of Unitarian Universalist churches and other inclusive settings, their naturalist perspectives can be valued.

Spiritual involvement in non-religious groups

Some naturalists are active in groups that are not overtly religious, but provide outlets for spiritual activity. Examples include working on ecologic or social justice initiatives, maintaining public gardens, working in food pantries, aiding the elderly, and participating in group kayak trips or nature walks. Each person who joins in can appreciate being active in something they care about and enjoy, and each (in their own way) may gain a sense of community or connection that can come from joining with others who have similar interests and values.

This can be seen in some overtly non-religious groups that provide opportunities for social connection. Examples have included the Sunday Assembly and a number of humanist, skeptic, atheist, and secular groups, including the Secular Student Alliance. While these groups may position themselves as anti-religious or as alternatives to religions, as they bring like-minded members together, they can also be seen as nontraditional ways of providing the types of involvement in a community that many have long appreciated as a part of being religious.

Some groups of naturalists and groups with focus on nature are listed in the Appendix.

Putting Values
into Practice

> "Surely it is the *way* a person lives and practices,
> or treats his neighbor or those in need,
> that is more expressive of religious living
> than the conventional markers of affiliation and action."
>
> — JAMES DAVIES

A close partner of developing religious attitudes is to act in ways that reflect one's values and beliefs. This can apply to personal morality (in acting with integrity, even when no one is watching), and attempts to contribute to a local community or the world at large.

One approach, suggested by a Buddhist friend, is simply to "help someone."

Some other examples include:

Values-based choices – in considering ecologic and social impact in purchases of food, clothing, energy, and cars; and by recycling and taking other steps to contribute, in small ways, to larger causes

(Some have described this as "eco-kosher," as it involves distinguishing actions that seem helpful and respectful from those that seem harmful or uncaring, and a moral mandate to try to act in ways that are good.)

Paying it forward (helping neighbors and ongoing courtesies to strangers)

Community service programs

Social activism (lobbying for public awareness or laws regarding ecologic balance, humane treatment of animals, or other causes)

While a goal can be to achieve positive outcomes, spiritual value can be gained through intent and activities. As Roger Gottlieb put it:

> "Although spiritual social activists … certainly want to win – pass the better law, overthrow the repressive regime, end discrimination – they also believe what they do has value even if they do not succeed. In standing for the moral truth as they see it, they have faith that they are embodying the same force of life and love that has brought them, and everything else, into existence…
>
> Even if a particular campaign or battle is lost … by some mysterious cosmic calculus, it matters what we do."

Part 3:
Questions and Challenges

With no view of an active God, an immortal soul, or related concepts, several topics that have long been considered in Western culture need to be looked at with different eyes.

Part 3 includes five chapters that examine some questions and challenges that may need to be addressed by those who look to nature.

A Natural Sense of Ourselves

Nature as a Focus of Religious Attention

Natural Values and Morality

Finding Hope, Strength, and Meaning

Personal Religious Orientation

A Natural Sense
of Ourselves

"There is no little man sitting in the mind somewhere
directing behavior of an individual.
Instead, the Self is a kind of center of narrative gravity,
a fiction, created by different regions of the brain
carrying out their normal information-processing operations."

— Patrick McNamara

A long-standing view in Western culture sees two parts of a human being – a physical body and an intangible soul. Modern science gives a different story, which raises questions and presents some challenges as we try to understand ourselves as biological beings.

If all that occurs in our bodies is the activity of molecules and cells, then what are thoughts and memories, and who, or what, am "I"?

If our choices and actions are often automatic or unconscious, how can we see ourselves as being in control – and is there such a thing as "free will"?

How can we reconcile our feeling of having an active "self" with the knowledge that this may be an illusion?

We don't ask these questions often, and we don't need to understand all of the inner workings of our brains (which is good, since much remains unknown). But, to increase our understanding of why we do the things we do and avoid problems that come with misconceptions, it's useful (and also interesting and, at times, a little strange) to draw from growing knowledge to form a sense of who we are.

Part of the challenge comes in recognizing that we are not one, but many things; and that our sense of ourselves can include elements from each.

From the perspective of biology, we can see ourselves as collections of cells, assembled as tissues and organs working together in body systems.

From the perspective of evolution, we can see ourselves as high-level primates; in sharing a genetic history of having emerged from forms of single-cell life, with aspects of body and mind (and wants, needs, and behaviors) that are present in other creatures, along with distinctive qualities of being human.

With a (partial) understanding of brain function and psychology, we can see our selves as originating in our brains, with general patterns of perceiving, interpreting, considering, and deciding that we share with other humans, plus individual patterns that form our own distinctive personalities.

These perspectives are parts of what we may see when we consider ourselves objectively – as a scientist, looking outside in, might try to explain what's occurring.

But, if we flip to a subjective/first-person/inside-out perspective of how it seems to us to be, we get an additional picture – of a self – "me" – looking out through eyes, viewing images, having thoughts, making choices, and directing a body through actions;

and thinking back on the past and planning for or wondering about the future.

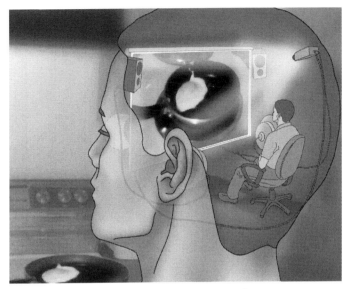

How it seems, to us, to be
(first-person/individual/subjective)
Adapted from an image created by Jennifer Garcia

Although we have learned to view our mind as a product of our brain, we also have a sense of mind and body as separate.

"I" hold up a finger and command it to bend, and watch as "it" responds.
(Try this, now, to be reminded of how it seems.)

The body can also feel like "other" when it fails to respond to our mental commands (for example, with injury or aging, where the mind is willing but a bum leg is holding us back).

We may also have a sense, which some have described as an illusion, that "I" can focus my thoughts on whatever "I" choose.

But as we understand that our minds are not separate from our brains, we may also, as a metaphor, accept a type of image – of a "self" (me) who, as in the idea of a spirit or soul or "ghost in the machine," is something other than a collection of cells, and represents a coherent and durable mental presence – without substance, but intelligent and (often) aware – that gives a way of envisioning ourselves as unique individuals.

Who are we?

What are we?

There are many facets to the whole.

Beyond collections of organs and cells, we are home to millions of microorganisms.

Looking deeper, we are a collection of atoms – each of which is composed of particles that trace back to the beginning of the cosmos, and each of which was previously part of many things.

We are a template (directed by DNA); where, as cells in our bodies die, new cells are formed and take their place, so that, over days and months and years, most of the substance in our bodies changes but the patterns and functions remain.

We are a point in an individual trajectory ("The child is father of the man"); where, over a lifespan we progress from conception to gestation, infancy, childhood, adolescence, adulthood, decline, death, and decomposition.

We are a point in an ancient trajectory; as the bearer of genetic and learned history that stretches back through ancestors to prehumans, and can continue through our own descendants.

We can also, at times, see ourselves as parts of a great cosmic dance – where, as Buddhists seek to realize, and as may occur at times in meditation or as we join in song at concerts or social-action marches or other unifying events, we may have a sense of having no self that is separate from other selves, and of melding with many as one. Or, as was discussed in *The Tao of Physics*, we may at times not even focus on our human selves and may briefly see ourselves as one of many fleeting combinations of interactions among particles and energy that have been occurring for billions of years, and that are now assembled in particular forms – us – that act in certain ways, and then in time break apart to become parts of other things.

We are parents, siblings, students, teachers, coworkers, teammates, neighbors, friends and other things – as parts of who we are involve relationships and roles.

On occasions when we stop to reflect, we can each see ourselves as these and other things.

Nature as a Focus
of Religious Attention

"The problem with nature being considered
as the object of religious devotion ...
is that nature does not exhibit
unqualified moral goodness."

— Donald Crosby

"Should we worship the morally ambiguous?
Should we worship anything less?"

— Jerome Stone

Part of the challenge of looking to nature as a focus of religious
attention is that the natural world is often (to our eyes) harsh,
with no concern for individuals. Amid creation is destruction, and
along with beauty are things that we respond to as horrible. Some
have asked that, if this is what we look to as a focus of religious
attention, how can we find comfort or consolation or reasons for
hope; and how can we envision, relate to, or take guidance from
impersonal natural processes?

We don't expect the cosmos to be concerned with our well-being.
But, as an order can be seen in the natural world – timeless and
powerful, with principles that are constant, and as the source of

all creation – we can appreciate this as awe-inspiring and regard it with reverence. As the reason why things are as they are and why things happen as they do, nature is of ultimate importance; and something we may engage with and learn from and try to understand and act in harmony with.

Envisioning nature

> "The Tao gives rise to all forms,
> yet it has no form of its own.
> If you attempt to fix a picture of it in your mind,
> you will lose it."
>
> — HUA HU CHING

It's one thing to say we look to nature. It's another thing to have a sense of what we have in mind as we speak of this.

So, as some think of God as "heavenly father" – having some qualities, like love, that we can imagine, and also being more than we can imagine – how might nature be envisioned as a focus of religious attention?

Is it in the expressions of nature we see – the flowers and trees, the ocean and sky?

Is it the principles that underlie these things, partly described as natural laws, where something in the nature of matter includes the potential to combine in ways that result in stars and planets and life?

Is it a combination of these, or something else?

An active, ordered, creative force can be seen. Whatever images we form are based on knowledge we have. So, as many of us can base a sense of what may be on what remains from what we learned in high school science, some have a deeper understanding of physics or biochemistry that can offer more sophisticated images. But all share a sense of mystery; where, beyond the limits of what is known lies much that we cannot understand.

Some Eastern philosophies and native traditions give perspectives that can be parts of what we may imagine. For example:

Tao considers the ways of nature, with varied elements in balance, and where apparent opposites can be complementary aspects of the same reality.

The Hindu concept of Brahman represents the creative principle that is expressed in all things in the world.

In some native American, Celtic, pantheist, and pagan views, the divine can be seen as present in rivers, trees, and other natural settings.

Some look to images of "Mother Earth" or "Gaia," where ecosystems are interrelated in ways that can let the whole planet be seen as a type of "superorganism."

Some envision energy fields on atomic or particle levels.

In Jewish, Christian and Islamic traditions the creative force is envisioned as God (including some views that do not include a personal presence).

The point in this is not to suggest a particular image, but to show that many types of images and combinations of images, some ancient and some more modern, offer ways of considering the forces and principles that cause things to be as they are – in ways that are consistent with the view that all that occurs is due to processes of nature.

Relating to or feeling connected to nature

> "The universe is no longer a mere *It* to us,
> it is a *Thou*, if we are religious;
> and any relation that may be possible
> from person to person
> might be possible here."
>
> — WILLIAM JAMES

Many authors have described ways of relating to, and feeling part of or one with nature. Some of this looks cosmic and ancient, in seeing ourselves as current configurations of energy that has been present for billions of years. Some is focused here on Earth, in coming to appreciate what we share with all living things.

But, while some images may prompt a sense of connection, nature can also seem distant, mechanical, impersonal, abstract, and uncaring.

We don't need to feel that nature is always holding us in a loving embrace. But if we are to regard nature as a focus of religious attention, some relation needs to be found between "me" and "it." And, if we see ourselves as part of or connected to nature, we may ask if some moral obligations might come with this, and what we should do in response.

With some parallels to what was discussed in the previous chapter, it can seem that "I" am right here and "it" is out there, all around – in what I can see, and in what lies in the distance beyond, and in the sky and the sea and the soil and the plants, and in all I can imagine on this planet, and in all that may exist throughout the cosmos.

We can also feel that "it" *is* "me," and I am an expression of it, as it is all of what I am – in my organs and brain, my blood and cells, and the molecules and atoms these are made of, and the ways these interact, which makes me alive and aware.

As in ways of considering God, it is immanent – present, here, in specific objects and creatures that we can touch and see; and it is transcendent – as the creative force that causes all things to be as they are.

It is not a being. It has no awareness of events. But it is steady, eternal, powerful – constant in some things, unpredictable in others; and, also, knowable in some ways, and unknowable in others.

Most of the time, our sense of nature can be vague – as simply the backdrop to settings in which we move.

Or, as has been described by a number of nature writers and mystics, aspects of nature can, at times, come into sharp focus; with responses that can range from the simple pleasure of noticing something beautiful to moments where we might lose our selves and feel part of all that is.

Taking guidance from the natural world

> "A central task of culture should be to remind us
> that the laws of nature apply to us
> as well as to trees, clouds and cliff faces."
>
> *The Book of Life*

While attention to nature can ground us with a sense of how things are, it does not directly show what we should do. And, as we look for lessons that might be drawn from observation of the natural world, some of what we see can seem troubling or contradictory.

No collections of stories or proverbs have been assembled into a naturalist bible. But a number of us have our own (mostly informal) collections; where, as we remember particular stories of animal behavior, or principles in biology, or findings from psychology studies, these can serve much like parables in the Bible, giving memorable, simple, metaphoric ways of shining light on small parts of a complex world.

Analogies from nature have a long history in religious traditions – as Jesus talked about seeds to illustrate virtues that might contribute to spiritual growth, and as Taoist writings point to nature to show qualities that we humans might aspire to. For example:

> "Nothing in the world is as soft and yielding as water. Yet for dissolving the hard and inflexible, nothing can surpass it."

This is also part of general culture, where the genres of nature writing and nature films provide many beautiful, moving, and insightful images of what occurs (in varied forms of life throughout the planet, and at levels from subatomic particles to galaxies), with implicit or explicit thoughts on how aspects of nature might apply to our lives.

Perspectives from nature can remind us of cycles, limits, and requirements – as we see a tree trunk decaying on a forest floor with a sapling growing nearby, or as we watch leaves fall from trees in autumn and know that with this change of season, we too, will change the pace of what we do and endure the winter cold before we'll again feel the warmth and flowering of spring.

Stories can reinforce ideals; where, as a nature film shows a newborn elephant struggling to climb up a bank after crossing a river, and not just its mother but also others in the herd use their trunks to lift it up, we can see that cooperation and care are not just human ideals, but are present in many species.

Some analogies involve considering nature in context with traditional religious themes, for example, as in this quote from Karl Peters:

> "How then can we live in harmony with nature? It is not simply living peacefully with sweet breezes and fresh water ... It does not mean promoting death, destruction, pain, and suffering ... Living in harmony with cruciform nature means being open to the possibilities of new life, new truth, new beauty, and new love that emerge in the midst of suffering."

We can also recognize cautionary tales, where circumstances such as too many rats in a cage can tip social life from tranquil to murderous.

Many examples have become common – with birds leaving the nest or learning to fly, industrious beavers, cooperative ants, sunrise and new beginnings, rain as nourishing and cleansing, a caterpillar transformed to a butterfly, and that a leopard can't change its spots. These and many other types of images can contribute to a loose collage of impressions that affect how we see and respond to the world.

Some care is warranted, as what is observed may be anthropomorphized, misunderstood, or interpreted in ways that forward an agenda. But, with that acknowledged, and to a point, some poetic license can have a place. As they give memorable examples of principles at work in nature, and of consequences that may follow types of actions, nature-based stories can contribute to ways of understanding and appreciating our lives and world, with insights that can help us respond to questions and challenges.

Natural Values
and Morality

"Is that which the gods love good because they love it,
or do they love it because it is good?"

— PLATO

"We want to understand how best to be good.
We want to know what to say to our children."

— URSULA GOODENOUGH AND PAUL WOODRUFF

Many people fear that, without belief in God, there is no basis for values, no source of moral guidance, and no incentive for ethical behavior. Based on this, they are often suspicious of nonbelievers.

Evidence shows that there's no basis for this fear. Naturalists are as law-abiding and moral as those who align with traditional religions. Values are consistent with those in our general cultures and the customs and laws of our communities. The Golden Rule is respected as part of a foundation for moral behavior. Honesty, courage, fairness, compassion, and a range of other virtues are appreciated as ideals.

But, without a recognized source of values, it's fair to ask:

Why should we be good?

What makes something good?

And, when faced with a moral dilemma, what standard can be used to determine what seems best?

Good answers exist, and are related to recognizing that values are part of what it means to be alive and morality is needed in all human groups.

A natural basis for values

Throughout most of the cosmos, there are no values. As galaxies swirl, stars "burn," and atoms combine to form molecules, there is no purpose or intent, no sense of benefit or harm, and no basis for judging events as good or bad.

But since living beings act in ways that enable them (or their species) to survive, from the perspective of these creatures, things that contribute to survival can be seen as good, while those that hinder well-being can be seen as bad. And as all living beings, even single-cell microorganisms, approach and interact with things that may contribute to their well-being, they can be said to value these things.

Although only humans are able to frame these distinctions in language, from the perspective of a living being it is better to be healthy than ill or in pain, and it is good to act in ways that do not lead to destruction. And with this, we can recognize a basis for values that is shared by creatures and cultures around the world; where, as individuals, we value physical and psychic well-being, and we value smooth and beneficial function in the groups to which we belong.

We also value things that contribute to well-being, such as the air, food, and water that sustain us and the types of behaviors that can help us or our groups to be healthy.

These values are not subjective (chosen by individuals). They are not fickle (as things we might change our minds about). They are present for all living things. And they are of ultimate concern. For, without survival, there would be no beings for whom it matters whether life is maintained, and no perspectives from which to consider values.

> With this, when setting goals or when considering what seems best in particular situations, being well – a "good life" and the preservation of healthy groups – can be held as a value and standard for action; and

> if well-being is appreciated as a core value, then we *ought* to act in ways that may help to achieve it.

A natural basis for morality

Morality is based in the fact that we are social beings. One of the keys to human success has been an ability to cooperate, and what we call morality is thought to have emerged as a combination of instincts and learned rules that contribute to the effective functioning of groups.

In contrast to a long-standing view of humans as naturally sinful or depraved, important aspects of moral behaviors appear to be innate; as can be seen in parents caring for their children despite sacrifice to themselves, and in expressions of empathy, a sense of fairness, and a willingness to help others. Some aspects of these traits can be seen in human infants, and also in chimpanzees, dolphins, elephants, and some other creatures.

Rules are present in interactions in social groups for primates, wolves, and some other species. These rules define what is allowed and what is prohibited or required, and occasions when exceptions can be made – for sharing food, mating, and other behaviors. The rules are taught to the young, and are enforced and reinforced as group members are rewarded or punished for acceptable or unacceptable behavior.

Moral standards are present – and similar – in human cultures around the world. All have rules against stealing, murder, and other acts that disrupt the cohesion of groups. As Steven Pinker describes it, when anthropologists survey moral concerns in varied cultures, "a few themes keep popping up from amid the diversity. People everywhere, at least in some circumstances and with certain other folks in mind, think it's bad to harm others and good to help them. They have a sense of fairness: that one should reciprocate favors, reward benefactors and punish cheaters. They value loyalty to a group, sharing and solidarity among its members and conformity to its norms. They believe that it is right to defer to legitimate authorities and to respect people with high status."

But, while general principles, like fairness and justice, are universal, specific examples of what is seen as right or wrong can vary by culture and subculture. For example, while all groups have standards for proper dress, particular views of what is proper can range from burkas to bikinis. An analogy has been made to language, where moral intuitions, like the ability to learn to speak, are innate in all human beings, but the particular languages we speak, like the particular rules for proper behavior, are taught to us and vary by culture.

Some potential implications of these views

As part of his "Atheism 2.0" TED talk, Alain de Botton discussed a difference between religion and education. Education, he said, presumes that, after something is taught, people know it. But religions know that people forget. So, for important ideas and moral lessons, they give regular reminders, by re-telling stories, pointing to role models, involving members in charitable projects, and discussing ways of applying ideals to our lives.

A challenge for naturalists is to find ways to grow in our ability to respond to moral questions, and to teach and coach and remind and involve our children.

One part of this can involve considering priorities among values. Since we can't give full attention to all of the attitudes or behaviors that most people agree are virtues, naturalists might identify particular values that can be recognized as priorities. So, as Buddhists emphasize compassion, and as Christians emphasize faith, love, forgiveness, and care for those in need, many naturalists, with life as a central value, see preservation of ecosystems as essential. Some other priority values may include:

knowledge (or seeking truth, as best it can be ascertained, with the scientific method as a respected approach);

humility (regarding the limits of our knowledge and capability);

gratitude (appreciation of our lives and all we have); and

humane treatment of animals (as fellow sentient beings).

Finding Hope,
Strength, and Meaning

"Every viable system of religious beliefs and practices …
must have *at its heart* ways of interpreting
and responding to the tragic dimensions of life
and of providing hope, strength, and meaning … "

— Donald Crosby

No one escapes the loss of loved ones. And most of us have times when we feel uncertain, alone, anxious, afraid, or that there is no point in what we do.

One role religions play is to frame these types of challenges in context with beliefs and offer practices that may help people to cope. Some of this can include mythic images (of wrestling with demons, gifts from angels, or insights from bodhisattvas) and showing paths where, in digging deep and finding strength, we may find solid footing that can help us in times of present and future troubles.

For Christians and Jews, these types of challenges are seen in context with a relationship with God.

In Buddhism, suffering is seen as due to selfish craving, and a solution is the 8-fold path.

A challenge for naturalists is to find ways to see our individual struggles as parts of what is normal in the natural world, in ways that may lead to a balance between striving and acceptance.

Purpose and meaning

"The more the universe seems comprehensible,
the more it seems pointless."

— Steven Weinberg

"Things do not matter in and of themselves,
but only through the attention we bring to them
and the love we bear them."

— André Comte-Sponville

With no view that we were created for a reason or that there might be eternal value in what we do, a naturalist view can be seen as cold and bleak. Some extend this to an image of Sisyphus or to a cosmic dimension, where in time the Sun will burn out, the human species will be extinct, and all presumed achievements will be gone.

But while there may be no ultimate purpose, meaning can be sought, and often found, by looking closer to home – to families, friends, and our communities, and also to ourselves; where it can matter a lot if we act in ways that are caring and helpful.

None of this is lasting, but it can matter here and now. And, we can extend this to hope for the future; where, as it is part of human nature to care for our children, with a "credo of continuation," we can try to contribute in ways that may help those who will come after us.

It may be a cliché, but it has also been shown in studies to be true – that, by giving, we receive. And as can be seen in quotes below from Viktor Frankl and Paul Tillich:

"… the meaning of life differs from man to man, from day to day and from hour to hour. What matters, therefore, is not the meaning of life in general but rather the specific meaning of a person's life at a given moment."

"What was really needed was a fundamental change in our attitude toward life… Our question must consist, not in talk and meditation, but in right action and in right conduct. Life ultimately means taking the responsibility to find the right answer to its problems and to fulfill the tasks which it constantly sets for each individual."

"Is there a courage which can conquer the anxiety of meaninglessness and doubt?"

"The act of accepting meaninglessness is in itself a meaningful act."

"A man who becomes conscious of the responsibility he bears toward a human being who affectionately waits for him, or to an unfinished work, will never be able to throw away his life. He knows the 'why' for his existence … "

Alienation

"I am a forty-two-year-old woman.
I've never received a love letter, never received flowers from a man.
I have attempted suicide and have contemplated it many times since.
And yet these wonders I have known:
a maple tree in autumn, each leaf exactly the color of gold;
a weed-like microcosm whose perfect petals are no bigger than the head of a pin.
The dawning of each season with its own unique perfume,
spring and autumn bringing the strongest scents.
These and many other moments of grace have kept me going."

— An unnamed woman, quoted by Sam Keen

Many of us have times when we feel invisible or alone; or out of touch with or in conflict with ourselves.

Psychologists and philosophers point to virtues that may contribute to finding a sense of belonging, with

courage	to confront challenges;
responsibility	for our choices; and
authenticity	in acting in ways that are consistent with who we are and what we value.

Another approach is more holistic and emotional; where, alongside problematic personal or social situations, we may find ways to feel that, as Fritjof Capra described it, "We belong to the universe, we are at home in it ..." Some come to a sense of belonging after random (or, sometimes, meditative or drug-induced) experiences in which we may feel part of nature. As one person described it: "I had the sense that I was intimately connected to everything – the sky, the trees, the grass,... the garden walls." And, after having been introduced to the potential to feel this type of connection, some learn to shift focus, when desired, to continue to embrace the world through these eyes.

Some approaches can be learned. For example, Michael Hogue described how we can see ourselves as separate-from, interacting-with, or parts-of all that is – by looking in different ways at what occurs. To illustrate, he described how, as he watched a rain cloud blowing toward him across a lake, he had the experience of being:

of nature –	as one of many separate entities, watching the approaching cloud as something other than himself; then

in nature –	interacting with the weather, as changing wind and darkened sky drew his attention and made him feel apprehensive; and then
as nature –	where, when he (and the grass and soil beneath him and the birds above) all became enveloped and soaked-through wet, he felt that he was part of the cloud.

While perceptions that lead to alienation may be real, these can be seen as only part of total reality. Our connection to all in nature is also real. At our core, each atom and cell in our bodies is part of the interconnected web of all that is. We are each fleeting parts/incarnations of something larger and more lasting than ourselves.

With some parallels to a theist view (that "this world" and "this life" are fleeting and of less consequence than the whole of creation) and with some parallels to a Buddhist view (that what we see as "self" is partly illusion, and that focus on self is a source of suffering), as a counterpoint to alienation, a naturalist option can be to hold images in our minds of all that we are connected to and part of.

Mortality

"In moments of grief – deep grief -
the only consolation you can find
is in the natural world."

— David Attenborough

Nothing grabs us more fully than the fact that life ends.

An important role of religions has been to help people cope with mortality – in describing what happens and why, to help us prepare and find ways to accept, and through community and ritual acts, to help us cope with loss.

A naturalist sense of what happens, and why

With a naturalist view, life ends at death. The body stops functioning when vital organs fail. And, with no view of a soul as a separate entity, when the brain ceases to function, nothing of the person remains – to have eternal life in heaven, or to be reborn in some other form, or to know "what it's like" to be dead.

The changes from birth to maturation and decline in aging are clear for all to see. But the how and why of it is understood mainly by biologists.

Ursula Goodenough gave an explanation that many have appreciated – in pointing to a step in evolution where, after more than a billion years when the only forms of life were single cells, a series of mutations occurred that enabled the emergence of multi-cellular forms of life that later evolved to become the many species we see today. As different types of cells enabled complex body functions, a major distinction emerged between:

germ cells (female eggs and male sperm), which enable reproduction; and

soma cells (which differentiate to become hearts, bones, brains, and many other types of cells, and perform coordinated functions that enable the body to remain alive until male and female germ cells can combine and reproduce).

After supporting reproduction, these soma cells serve no further function for the long-term continuance of the species; and their structure is such that, over the course of a lifespan, due to errors in DNA replication and other causes, they become slower, weaker, and less capable over time, until they can no longer enable organs to function properly, and the being dies.

"And it is here," Goodenough said, "that we arrive at one of the central ironies of human existence. Which is that our sentient brains are uniquely capable of experiencing deep regret and sorrow and fear at the prospect of our own death, yet it was the invention of death, the invention of the germ/soma dichotomy, that made possible the existence of our brains."

In this, we might take some consolation in understanding the biological reality – that the processes that enable our lives require that we must die.

A sense that something may continue

The transformation of death – from active and vital, to gone – is strange and hard to grasp.

A sense of the "spirit" of the deceased may continue – in memories and emotional responses (for example, to a photograph, a letter, or a bench that someone made, like the mental image of a living friend who we haven't seen in years). We can recognize these as impressions in our brains but, as in cases when loved ones appear and speak to us in dreams, these images can also seem very real.

Many religions look at death as a point of transition, not an end. While the body no longer is living, a soul or spirit is thought to live on.

Naturalists have no belief that a particular self may continue. The person we knew is gone. But several images can give a sense that *something* may continue.

One image relates to the constancy in matter, and a view of ongoing transformation as part of nature. For example, when an individual ceases to live, its substance breaks apart, and new entities are formed from the parts.

If a body is buried beneath a tree and decomposes into the soil, the substance becomes part of the tree. That matter continues and transforms further, as leaves are eaten by caterpillars, which in turn are eaten by birds, and material substance that was once a person passes on over time to become part of many other things.

> Ashes to ashes, dust to dust …
> Individual forms are fleeting, but the process continues.
> Nothing is lost. All things reconfigure …
> Not a continuation of self, but a continuation of the processes and activity that created our self.

Another perspective is genetic legacy, with continuation through our children and descendants. Part of our personal essence is encoded in DNA. With this, some traits we have – some parts of who we are – are passed on to our children and their children.

Also, with organ transplantation, some part a person can live on.

A related view is personal legacy, where things we teach and ways we influence others may continue – for a while. Like ripples on a pond after a stone is thrown in, these fade away over time.

But, apart from ripples fading, something occurs in every life. And with the "butterfly effect" as an image, we can see how a life, each life, is part of a sequence of events that, had it not been there, would have had a different trajectory. The individual may not live on, but the presence and actions of the person affected all that follows. The effect may be subtle and small. But, if this particular life had not been lived, things now and in the future would be different.

An additional view includes a symbolic sense of unity. One part of this is in "joining" others who have passed.

Whatever has become of what was once their "spirit" or individual personal presence will also happen to us.

As they are now spared the struggles of the world, when our time comes, so will we.

Appreciation of endings

> "a serenity is on offer
> in letting go of the concept of endlessness"
>
> — Ursula Goodenough

Another part of making peace with death can be getting to a place of accepting that, as all things in the cosmos change, all specific living things must come to an end. (This can be related to the Buddhist ideal of non-attachment). This view is easiest to hold when responding to the death of an elderly person who had lived a good life (particularly if they had declined and suffered toward the end). It can be much harder to hold when responding to a fatal accident or the death of a child. And, as we attempt to apply this to thoughts about our own deaths, and as we consider the naturalist view in contrast to the idea of going to heaven, the question can be asked:

are we just rationalizing, or pretending that endings are ok, or do we truly, not begrudgingly, deep-down actually believe this?

One point of reference can be to think through the idea of eternal life. Beyond "is it plausible?", we might ask "is this desirable?" Is this something that, if we had the option, we'd actually want? As some ancient myths and modern stories and films have shown, even if such a thing could occur, eternal bliss may not seem as blissful over time.

One perspective on this was described by Alan Watts, who said:

> "The secret of the enjoyment of pleasure is to know when to stop ...
> We do this every time we listen to music. We do not seize hold of a particular chord or phrase and shout at the orchestra to go on playing it for the rest of the evening; on the contrary. However much we may like that particular moment of music, we know that its perpetuation would interrupt and kill the movement of the melody. We understand that the beauty of a symphony is less in these musical moments than in the whole movement from beginning to end. If the symphony tried to go on for too long, if at a certain point the composer exhausts his creative abilities and tries to carry on just for the sake of filling in the required space of time, then we begin to fidget in our chairs, feeling that he has denied the natural rhythm, has broken the smooth curve from birth to death, and that though a pretense of a life is being made, it is in fact a living death...
> we have to learn the art of enjoying things *because* they are impermanent."

Personal Religious Orientation

Unlike much of history, when religion was required or was a social norm, being religious is now (for many) an option that we can engage with or not as we choose. Many do so in what has been called a "cafeteria-style"; where, often drawing from a range of traditions, we can each decide for ourselves which practices and views to adopt, adapt, or reject.

This general trend in modern religion is magnified for naturalists; where, with no established dogma and few in-person groups, we aren't just able, but are mostly required to set our own paths for exploration. If we want to learn and grow, we each need to identify our own priorities and interests and find our own resources and approaches. When looking for guidance, counseling, or discussion of ideas, we each need to find companions or communities.

This gives freedom that many find attractive. But it also raises some questions – in how (or when, or whether) to consider religious questions, and which approaches seem best for religious focus, religious language, and religious identity.

Religious focus

With many avenues that can be explored, and with limits to our interests and time, if we're to engage the spiritual parts of ourselves in independent ways, we may ask:

What do I feel drawn to, or what might I like to gain from involvement with religious questions or activities?

Am I looking for mystical moments, or ways of becoming wiser or more appreciative or giving, or in exploring some other aspect of spirituality?

Some answers can be shaped by time of life. When we are young, we might have questions and focus on learning, and as we grow old (among other things), we may look for ways to cope with loss. And, overall, as was discussed in the Practices section, our spiritual attention can be directed at personal growth, orienting our minds, religious attitudes, or putting our values into practice.

There's no need to set a path or make a conscious plan. But if we're interested in an orientation that requires some self-direction, it can be useful, at times, to consider what we do – and what we don't do, and what we might like to do more of – as parts of our own personal ways of being religious.

One aspect of this is the question of:

What relation, if any, do I want with traditional religions?

Many reach the point where it seems best to step away from the religion they were raised with. But, as part of this, many also feel that, while we may view some ancient teachings as outdated or wrong, we can also recognize insights and wisdom. And, as we can respect what's been learned as religions have considered important questions (in ways that were shaped by their cultures and times), some advise against "throwing babies out with the bathwater," and being open to appreciating the value that can remain.

For those who agree with this general concept, more questions are raised – about which aspects of traditions might be kept.

What stories might we continue to tell? What poems, proverbs, prayers?

Which teachers and leaders might we look to as role models?

For those who disagree, the question shifts to:

What modern stories and role models might be used, instead – to inform or inspire?

Outcomes from this can vary – from naturalists who have little interest in (or might actively oppose) traditional religious approaches; to naturalists who are active members of Christian, Jewish, Buddhist, or other religious communities; plus naturalists who draw pieces from a number of modern ideas and ancient traditions.

Religious language

When considering religious ideas (even from naturalist perspectives), it can be hard to avoid using words that are associated with traditional religions. This brings the question of determining which of these we may sometimes see as useful and which we mostly prefer not to use.

Might we feel "reverence" toward nature?

Can the life of a child be seen as "sacred"?

Should we speak of a person's "spirit" or "soul"?

Might some people, places, or things be referred to as "holy"?

Do we have "faith" in what we believe?

Have we had feelings of something "numinous" or "transcendent"?

Can we talk about a "heaven" or "hell"?

Many of these terms have several definitions – some of which are not religious. Lack of clarity can occur if we choose to use them – or if we use them as metaphors when speaking with people who see them as actual. But lack of clarity can also occur no matter what we choose, as all words for abstract ideas are, by their nature, imprecise.

One option, as is often done with songs that are sung in Humanist or Unitarian Universalist gatherings, is to replace religious language with similar, more secular, terms. Some like this as a way of keeping some aspects of messages and tradition. Others feel that, as it strips out symbols and poetry, emotional feeling is lost – to a point of no longer seeming worth using.

Another option is to be selective – and to generally avoid some words, but to be comfortable using others, and decide which terms to use case by case. We can also explain what we mean when we use religious terms in non-traditional ways.

Some religious words spark active debate. A prominent example is "God."

God language

While naturalists agree that there is no "guy in the sky" that may affect specific events by causing miracles, a number use the term God as a metaphor. Like Albert Einstein, they may make it clear that "I cannot conceive of a God who rewards and punishes his creatures, or has a will of the type of which we are conscious in ourselves," but some may also use God as a way of referring to the forces that cause all things to be as they are.

Some use God as Stuart Kauffman did (as a symbol for the creative potential in nature); or as Paul Tillich did (as "ground of being"); or as Nancy Abrams describes – as a symbol constructed by humans that can be seen as "real" (in the sense that Ebenezer Scrooge and ideals of love and freedom can be seen as real) – in being examples or ideas that can affect what we aspire to and do. And some feel it can be useful to use the term "God" in conversations with believers, to indicate common ground in respect for life and a grounding in morals.

A number of naturalists disagree. They do not themselves use the term "God," and they may object to others using this term, feeling that naturalist usage can be misunderstood or misleading, or that it helps to perpetuate a fiction that they'd like to see decline.

Religious identity

A final question is how those of us with a naturalist worldview might describe our religious orientation.

Many like and use the term "religious naturalist" to affirm an attitude or belief that there are religious aspects of this world that can be appreciated within a naturalistic framework.

Some prefer "spiritual" to "religious" and may describe themselves as "spiritual naturalists," or "spiritual atheists," or "spiritual but not religious."

Some don't want to highlight a religious or spiritual sense, and may describe themselves simply as "naturalist."

Some use "secular" to declare an active lack of interest in things religious. Or, some just say they have "no religion."

Some use "pantheist" to convey a reverence for nature or a way of seeing nature as identical to God, or "pagan" to describe how they relate spiritually to particular aspects of nature).

Some use "atheist," "agnostic," "skeptic," or "freethinker" to point to how their views compare to the beliefs of Western religions.

Some describe themselves as "Humanist," as distinct from being "religious," to affirm a lifestance "guided by reason, inspired by compassion, and informed by experience" that "encourages us to live life well and fully."

Among those who were raised in Christian, Jewish, or other religious communities, many identify with these traditions, regardless of what they believe about God or other teachings, or whether or not they remain actively involved.

Some use multiple terms and might say that they are Christian naturalist, Jewish Humanist, or part Buddhist and part pagan or mystic (or some other combination). In this, some give weighted emphasis, saying they're mainly A, with bits of B and C.

Many try to avoid using labels.

In many ways, names are not important. But, as we recognize connotations that come with different terms, and if we consider these with respect to our own leanings, we can clarify ways in which we see ourselves as spiritual/religious (or not); and, if asked, we can draw from available terms to convey what we'd like others to understand.

Wrap-up: What it Can Mean to Look to Nature

"After you have exhausted what there is
in business, politics, conviviality, love, and so on —
have found that none of these finally satisfy,
or permanently wear —
what remains?
Nature remains;
to bring out from their torpid recesses,
the affinities of a man or woman with the open air,
the trees, fields, the changes of seasons —
the sun by day and the stars of heaven by night."

— WALT WHITMAN

After an overview of topics that are parts of an emerging whole, we'll return to a theme and a question that were introduced at the start – in what can it mean to look to nature as a focus of religious attention.

Answers can be considered from several perspectives, in what it can mean ...

personally   to each of us, ourselves;

socially   in how these views may contribute to our
                 cultures; and

globally   in ways that naturalist attitudes, values, and
              actions may contribute to balanced long-
              term well-being.

When we consider this personally, looking to nature can mean
forming a way of understanding that gives a foundation from
which to consider important questions, with no conflict between
what can be understood through science and spiritual perceptions
and ideals.

It can mean having good reasons to spend time in natural settings; where we can be moved by and learn from the beauty,
order, and wonder in our world.

It can mean affirming that we care.

And it can mean feeling that we ought to act in ways that reflect
this.

When we consider social perspectives, looking to nature can mean
expanding options that people can consider for religious orientation, at a time when involvement in traditional religions is declining. It can also mean increased inclusion of perspectives that are
both naturalist and spiritual in discussion of moral issues and social policies – as a complement, and sometimes as a counterpoint,
to views that are supported by traditional religions.

Beyond personal and social perspectives, looking to nature can
mean thinking ecologically and globally, and recognizing that, as
all is interconnected, our ability to thrive is related to the well-being of the whole. This, in turn, can mean seeing all of the people
and creatures and ecosystems in the world as parts of what we
"take to heart."

It can mean imagining the type of world we'd like to see and the
steps that can be taken to work toward this.

Thomas Berry and others have described a potential future "heaven" – where, if we can learn and plan and change our ways, a balance may be found – among humans and other species and with approaches to social justice that can provide long-term well-being.

This also includes an image of a potential future "hell," where if changes are not made (or if we try but don't get it right), we may cause our own destruction, with social disruption, war, personal tragedies, and the devastation of natural environments.

This can add spiritual values to practical reasons for why we should work toward formation of a balanced, sustainable world that we'd like to leave to our children and those who follow.

None of this matters to nature.

But it matters to us.

As we seek our own well-being, and as we care for family and friends, and as we feel connected to and part of the creative order and beauty in nature, we can draw from naturalist values – to notice, appreciate, and learn – and try to act in ways that can enable this natural world, in balance, to continue.

Acknowledgements

This book is the product of a search for a personal way of being religious that draws from modern knowledge, appreciates ancient wisdom, and combines feelings and actions with ideas. It's a response to a time of change, where, if traditional approaches are seen as unappealing or unbelievable, we are forced to find or form our own ways. And in this we can learn from others who have also explored.

My introduction was Sunday School at a New England Congregational church, where I was intrigued by bible stories and a sparkling stained glass image of Jesus, and enjoyed the quiet mood on Sunday mornings when the bell rang out, as it had for 200 years, to call parishioners to service.

As a teen, I had questions that teachers from this tradition couldn't answer, which led to stepping away, and to exploration of Eastern and other traditions. And, when these, too, showed limits, the only option seemed to be a loose collage of impressions, with pieces drawn from varied perspectives.

This lay dormant for a while, until I had two boys who reached an age that prompted me to wonder, "What should I teach them?" I gathered and shared some stories. And while the boys showed little interest, my own interest was rekindled, which led to reading and taking notes, and then writing a book, *Einstein's God*, which used the views of this thoughtful, brilliant man as a focus for exploring a way of being spiritual that fit with what could be understood through science.

When the partial answers this provided led to deeper questions, I enrolled at the School of Theology at Boston University, and was surprised and pleased to see that approaches I'd been exploring were directions that a number of philosophers, theologians, psychologists, and others were also discussing. From this and all that followed, I'll state my appreciation to professors and fellow students for broadening my perspectives and presenting challenges to look deeper and consider how pieces may relate. This includes particular gratitude to Wesley Wildman who, in combining the best of both scholar and teacher, encouraged ways of respecting authors while also thinking critically, and pointed me to interesting groups of fellow explorers.

A valuable part of this was joining in active, in-depth discussions with members of the Institute on Religion in an Age of Science (IRAS). This led to me contributing to the Religious Naturalist Association (RNA) to help provide resources and support a growing community of people from a wide range of backgrounds in exploring ways of putting naturalist spiritual perspectives into practice. In both groups, ongoing conversations gave a rich trove of ideas and new friendships. It also led to further contact with people and groups, worldwide, with similar interests.

Among many people who have been important in this, I'll extend special thanks to Michael Cavanaugh who, from the start, has been welcoming and encouraging and has sparked a number of ideas. Special thanks, also, to Ursula Goodenough; who, along with substantial accomplishment, knowledge, and wisdom has always been warm and real; and has encouraged a focus on people, naturalists, moreso than ideas of naturalism, and who, when coaxed into a position of leadership, does so by example.

Beyond people I've come to know, many thanks to authors of books, articles, blogs, and other works that give insight into the varied topics that have been discussed here; and, also to artists, activists, and others who – each in their own ways – share some common interests and concerns.

Appreciation, also, to John Mabry, as publisher of Apocryphile Press, with a mission to provide "spiritual reading, on the edge."

And, thanks to friends and family who, over the years, have added to or endured conversations on these and many far-ranging topics. Thanks to Dan Lewis, Keith Lang, Dee Mallon, and others who gave the manuscript a reality-check and useful thoughts on focus and form. And many thanks to my wife, Robin – for patience and love, for bringing my head down out of the clouds, and for the great quality of enjoying the simple things.

Appendix

Being spiritual and religious (selected quotes)

"We come to life in this world,
marked by our evolutionary history
and heavily influenced by
impulses we do not fully understand
and by contexts we cannot fully control.
And it is in these circumstances that we strive
to discover meaning and purpose in our lives;
to build creative cultures and secure societies;
and to realize the good, the true, and the beautiful.

These are religious and spiritual activities,
and we work out our salvation,
our liberation, and our enlightenment
as we pursue them."

— Wesley Wildman —

"... religion is a way of life that involves many processes – all of which, in different ways, are directed to a common end. The goal is to reach a state of being that is conceived to be the highest possible state or condition."

— FREDERICK STRENG, CHARLES LLOYD, AND JAY ALLEN—

"A religious person ... may or may not self-identify with a religion. Rather, a religious orientation encompasses three spheres of human experience:

(1) The interpretive sphere (a.k.a. theological, philosophical, existential) describes responses to the Big Questions, such as,

Why is there anything at all rather than nothing?
Does the universe, or my life, have a Plan? a Purpose?
How do I come to terms with death?
Why is there evil and suffering?

(2) The spiritual sphere describes such inward personal responses to existence as gratitude, awe, humility, reverence, assent, transcendence, and at-oneness.

(3) The moral sphere describes outward communal responses such as care, compassion, fair-mindedness, responsibility, trust, and commitment."

— URSULA GOODENOUGH AND TERRENCE W. DEACON —

"If you have ever extended a simple kindness
when you are suffering yourself,
chosen to feel grateful rather than deprived,
understood how much we share
despite our differences of culture or ideology,
then even if you have never used the word,
you have a firsthand experience of spirituality ..."

— ROGER GOTTLIEB —

"Spirituality begins in movement –
away from what we come to see as unreal, painful, disappointing,
trivial, or meaningless
and toward the ultimate, true, vital, real, or sacred."

— ROGER GOTTLIEB —

"As taught by virtually every religious tradition
(though not always as their dominant message)
and as embraced by countless individuals ...
this is what we hear:
You are not who you think you are, and
you do not have to live the way you think you do."

— ROGER GOTTLIEB —

"The important difference between religious (spiritual) persons
and nonreligious (nonspiritual) persons
is a matter of attitudes."

— LOYAL RUE —

"Typical of religious outlooks and experiences
are an openness to and grateful reception of
unearned, unplanned, unexpected mercies and gifts …,
a sense of forgiveness and self-forgiveness for past wrongs
and new hope for the future."

— Donald Crosby —

"The religious attitude … accepts the objective truth
of two central judgments about value.

The first holds that
human life has objective meaning or importance…

The second holds that what we call "nature" –
the universe as a whole and all its parts –
is … something of intrinsic value and wonder."

— Ronald Dworkin —

"There are countless … ways in which
spiritual illumination may enter our lives.
But despite the different circumstances in which they arise,
they all share some common features:
acceptance of reality rather than resistance to it,
gratitude rather than greed for more,
compassionate connection to other people rather than isolation,
and
a profound, joyous, nongrasping enjoyment of life."

—Roger Gottlieb —

"William James said that:
Like love, like wrath, like hope, ambition, jealousy,
like every other instinctive eagerness and impulse
[religion] adds to life an enchantment
which is not rationally or logically deducible from anything else.
The enchantment is the discovery of transcendental value
in what seems otherwise transient and dead."

— RONALD DWORKIN —

"The universe is no longer a mere It to us,
it is a Thou, if we are religious;
and any relation that may be possible from person to person
might be possible here."

— WILLIAM JAMES —

"… the religious sensibility
opens up an expansive and inspiring vision
of the numinous world of which we humans are a part
and for whose continuing well-being
we have special responsibility."

— DONALD CROSBY —

"Were one asked to characterize the life of religion
in the broadest and most general terms possible,
one might say that it consists of the belief
that there is an unseen order,
and that our supreme good
lies in harmoniously adjusting ourselves thereto."

— WILLIAM JAMES —

"… religion means much more than a state of mind
or [an] ecstatic or mystical mood.
It's a commitment over a lifetime
to what a person considers to be good."

— JOHN HAUGHT —

"… to borrow a phrase from Jesus of Nazareth,
we'll be known by our fruit…
Our witness isn't what we say we believe
or even what we think we believe.
Neither is it the image, pose or posture
we try to present to others.
It's what we do, what we give, what we take
and what we actually bring to our little worlds."

— DAVID DARK —

"I am religious precisely because I make an effort
to live and act in deliberate, reflective accord
with my worldview."

— DAVID SIMONTON —

Groups of Naturalists and Groups with Focus on Nature

The list below shows a number of groups where aspects of community can be found, as they serve as focal points for joining with people with shared values and worldview – in caring about, relating to, and looking to learn from, enjoy, and preserve the natural world.

Additional information can be seen by viewing group websites.

Naturalist and actively spiritual/religious
Religious Naturalist Association (RNA)
Spiritual Naturalist Association
World Pantheism Movement
Society for Humanistic Judaism
Unitarian Universalist Religious Naturalists
The Clergy Project

Promoting understanding/acceptance of the story of evolution
National Science Teaching Association
Deep Time Journey Network
The Great Story

Nature appreciation
Camp Quest
Local hiking and canoe/kayak groups and garden clubs

Naturalist and exploring nontheist approaches to morality and well-being
Humanist Association
Secular Alliances
   Secular Student Alliance
   Ethical Culture
Atheist Alliance
Skeptics Society
Brights

Nature preservation
Sierra Club
Audubon Society
Nature Conservancy
Earth Day Network
Artists for the Earth
National Wildlife Federation
Friends of the Earth

References and Resources

The list below shows books and articles that provide information and ideas relating to topics that are discussed in this book.

Additional information and perspectives on these and related topics can be found at the Religious Naturalism website:

religiousnaturalism.org

which includes links to additional resources, including books and articles, TED talks, nature videos, NASA photographs, and museum displays, plus art, poetry, lectures, sermons, and other resources.

Abrams, Nancy Ellen. *A God That Could be Real: Spirituality, Science, and the Future of Our Planet.* Beacon Press. 2016.

American Humanist Association. *Humanism and Its Aspirations: Humanist Manifesto III.* American Humanist Association. 2003.

Barrett, Michael. "Is there a natural affinity between mindfulness, or other secular forms of meditation, and religious naturalism?" Essay posted at: religiousnaturalism.org.

Benson, Herbert with Klipper, Mariam. *The Relaxation Response.* William Morrow. 1975.

Bering, Jesse and Heywood, Bethany. "Do Atheists Reason Implicitly in Theistic Terms? Evidence of Teleo-Functional Biases in the Autobiographical Narratives of Nonbelievers." Abstract. *Society for Personality and Social Psychology 2010 Annual Meeting.* p. 32.

Berry, Thomas. "The Ecozoic Era." Eleventh Annual E. F. Schumacher Lectures. October 1991. Great Barrington, Massachusetts.

Braxton, Donald. "Religious Naturalism and the Future of Christianity." *Zygon.* 2007; 42(2): 317-342.

Brown, Lenora Inez. "Writing Religion: Is God a Character in Your Plays?" 2000. *American Theatre*; 17(9): 29-32.

Brown, Donald E. *Human Universals.* McGraw Hill. 1991.

Capra, Fritjof. *The Tao of Physics: An Exploration of the Parallels Between Modern Physics and Eastern Mysticism.* 25th Anniversary Edition. Shambhala Publications. 2000.

Capra, Fritjof. *The Hidden Connections: A Science for Sustainable Living.* Harper Collin. 2002.

Comins, Mike and Savage, Nigel. *A Wild Faith. Jewish Ways into Wilderness, Wilderness Ways into Judaism.* Jewish Lights Publishing. 2007.

Comte-Sponville, André. *The Little Book of Atheist Spirituality.* Viking. 2006.

Crosby, Donald A. *A Religion of Nature.* State University of New York Press. 2002.

Crosby, Donald A. *The Thou of Nature: Religious Naturalism and Reverence for Sentient Life.* State University of New York Press. 2013.

Crosby, Donald A. *More Than Discourse: Symbolic Expressions of Naturalistic Faith*. State University of New York Press. 2014.

Damasio, Antonio. *The Feeling of What Happens: Body and Mind in the Making of Consciousness*. Harcourt Brace. 1999.

Dark, David. *Life's Too Short to Pretend You're Not Religious*. IVP Books. 2016.

Davies, James. "The Rationalization of Suffering." *Harvard Divinity Bulletin*. 2011; 39(1-2): 49-56.

Dawkins, Richard. *Unweaving the Rainbow: Science, Delusion and the Appetite for Wonder. Houghton Mifflin. 1998.*

de Botton, Alain. Atheism 2.0. TEDGlobal 2011. July, 2011.

Deep Time Journey Network. *"The Cosmic Walk." Deeptime Network website.*

Dennett, Daniel. *Elbow Room: The Varieties of Free Will Worth Wanting*. MIT Press. 1984.

Dowd, Michael and Barlow, Connie. "Great Story Beads." The Great Story website (accessed 12-10-2019).

Dworkin, Ronald. *Religion Without God*, Harvard University Press. 2013.

Einstein, Albert. *The World As I See It. Philosophical Library. 1949.*

Einstein, Albert. *Ideas and Opinions. Modern Library. 1994.*

Emerson, Ralph Waldo. *Essays: First Series*. Munroe. 1841.

Eng, Karen. "On the 12 steps to a compassionate life: Q&A with Karen Armstrong." January 12, 2011. TED Blog website (accessed 12-10-2019).

Fitzpatrick, Liam. "The Art of Dying". *Time Magazine*. 2019; February: 4-11.

Fleischman, Paul R. *Wonder: When and Why the World Appears Radiant*. Small Batch Books. 2013.

Frankl, Viktor. *Man's Search for Meaning*. Pocket Books. 1985.

Goodenough, Ursula. "Biology: What One Needs to Know." 1996; *Zygon;* 31(4): 671–680.

Goodenough, Ursula. *The Sacred Depths of Nature*. Oxford University Press. 1998.

Goodenough, Ursula and Woodruff, Paul. "Mindful Virtue, Mindful Reverence." 2001. *Zygon;* 36: 585-595.

Goodenough, Ursula and Deacon, Terrance. "The Sacred Emergence of Nature." *The Oxford Handbook of Religion and Science*. Oxford University Press. 2008.

Goodenough, Ursula. "Are You A Religious Naturalist Without Knowing It?" *13.7 Cosmos and Culture*. January 29, 2010. National Public Radio (NPR) website (accessed 12-10-2019).

Goodenough, Ursula. "Who Is My "I-Self"? *13.7 Cosmos and Culture*. March 2, 2010. National Public Radio (NPR) website (accessed 12-10-2019).

Goodenough, Ursula. "My Covenant with Mystery." *13.7 Cosmos and Culture*. August 27, 2010. National Public Radio (NPR) website (accessed 12-10-2019).

Goodenough, Ursula. IRASnet. Group e-mail communication June 13, 2013.

Gottlieb. Roger. *Spirituality: What It Is And Why It Matters*. Oxford University Press. 2013.

Haidt, Jonathan. *The Righteous Mind: Why Good People Are Divided by Politics and Religion*. Vintage. 2013.

Hawking, Stephen and Mlodinow, Leonard. *The Grand Design*. Random House. 2012.

Hawking, Stephen. *A Brief History of Time: From the Big Bang to Black Holes*. Bantam. 1988.

Hogue, Michael S. *The Promise of Religious Naturalism*. Rowman & Littlefield. 2010.

Idler, Ellen. "The Psychological and Physical Benefits of Spiritual/Religious Practices." 2008. *Spirituality in Higher Education Newsletter*; 4(2).

James, William. *The Will to Believe*. An Address to the Philosophical Clubs of Yale and Brown Universities. 1896.

James, William. *The Varieties of Religious Experience*. Longmans, Green, and Co. 1902.

Kauffman, Stuart. "Beyond Reductionism: Reinventing the Sacred." *Edge.org*. Conversation: Culture. 11.12.2006.

Keen, Sam. *In the Absence of God: Dwelling in the Presence of the Sacred*. Harmony Books. 2010.

Louv, Richard. *Last Child in the Woods: Saving Our Children From Nature-Deficit Disorder*. Algonquin Books. 2008.

May, Gerald. *The Wisdom of Wilderness: Experiencing the Healing Power of Nature*. Harper One. 2007.

McDonnell, Alan R. "Giving really is better than receiving." *Psychology Today*. December 25, 2010.

McNamara, Patrick. *The Neuroscience of Religious Experience*. Cambridge University Press, 2009.

Mitchell, Stephen (translator). *Tao Te Ching by Lao Tzu*. Harper Perennial Modern Classics. 2006.

Mlodinow, Leonard. *The Drunkard's Walk: How Randomness Rules Our Lives*. Pantheon. 2008.

Moore, Thomas. *A Religion of One's Own*. Avery. 2015.

Muir, John. *My First Summer in the Sierra*. Houghton Mifflin. 1911.

Newberg, Andrew and Waldman, Mark Robert. *Why We Believe What We Believe: Uncovering Our Biological Need for Meaning, Spirituality, and Truth*. Free Press. 2006.

Peters, Karl. *Dancing with the Sacred: Evolution, Ecology, and God*. Trinity Press International. 2002.

Pew Research Center. "Many Americans Mix Multiple Faiths." Table: Religious or Mystical Experiences. *Pew Forum on Religion & Public Life*. 2009

Phares, Ron. Religious Naturalism: Balance. Sermon recorded on June 3, 2013.

Pinker, Steven. *The Blank Slate*. Penguin Books. 2003.

Pinker, Steven. "The Moral Instinct." *New York Times Magazine*. January 13, 2008.

Public Broadcast System (PBS). "Religion and the Brain." *Religion and Ethics Newsweekly*. November 9, 2001.

Raymo, Chet. *The Path: A One-Mile Walk Through the Universe*. Bloomsbury. 2004.

Ricardo, Alonzo and Szostak, Jack W. "Life on Earth." 2009. *Scientific American*; 301(3): 54-56.

Rojas, John-Paul Ford. "Sir David Attenborough's Comfort from Grief in Natural World". *The Telegraph*. October 11, 2011.

Roth, Gabrielle. "The Spiritual Power of Dance." Huff Post Blog. May 15, 2011.

Rue, Loyal D. *Religion Is Not About God: How Spiritual Traditions Nurture our Biological Nature and What to Expect When They Fail*. Rutgers University Press. 2004.

Rue, Loyal. *Nature is Enough: Religious Naturalism and the Meaning of Life*. State University of New York Press. 2012.

Sagan, Carl. *Pale Blue Dot: A Vision of the Human Future in Space*. Random House. 1994.

Sagan, Carl. *Cosmos*. Random House. 1980.

Schlauch, Chris. "Psychology of Religion: Retrospective." School of Theology, Boston University. 2013.

School of Life. "Chapter 5: Calm, The Lessons of Nature". *The Book of Life*. The School of Life website (accessed 12-10-2019).

Simonton, David. Personal essay. 2017. Posted at Religious Naturalist Association website.

Stone, Jerome A. "What Is Religious Naturalism?" 2000. *Journal of Liberal Religion*; 2: 60-74.

Stone, Jerome A. *Religious Naturalism Today: The Rebirth of a Forgotten Alternative*. SUNY Press. 2008.

Stone, Jerome A. "Spirituality for Naturalists." 2012. *Zygon*; 47(3): 481-500.

Streng, Frederick; Lloyd, Charles; Allen, Jay. *Ways Of Being Religious: Readings for a New Approach to Religion*. Prentice-Hall. 1973.

Strain, Daniel. "Naturalistic Spirituality as a Practice." Chapter 30 in *The Routledge Handbook of Religious Naturalism*. Edited by Donald A. Crosby and Jerome A. Stone. Routledge. 2018.

Tillich, Paul. *Systematic Theology Volume I*. University of Chicago Press. 1951.

Tillich, Paul. *The Courage to Be*. Yale University Press. 1952.

Vernon, Jamie L. "Understanding the Butterfly Effect." 2017. *The Scientist*; 105(3): 130.

Walker, Brian (translator). *Hua Hu Ching: The Unknown Teachings of Lao Tzu*. HarperOne. 2009.

Watts, Alan. *The Meaning of Happiness*. New World Library. 2018.

Weinberg, Steven. *The First Three Minutes: A Modern View of the Origin of the Universe*. Basic Books. 1993.

Whitman, Walt. *Specimen Days and Collect*. Rees Welsh and Company 1882.

Wildman, Wesley. *Religious and Spiritual Experiences*. Cambridge University Press. 2011.

Wilson, Edward O. *Biophilia: The Human Bond with Other Species*. Harvard University Press. 1984.

Wilson, Edward O. *On Human Nature: Twenty-fifth Anniversary Edition, With a New Preface*. Harvard University Press. 2004.

Wilson, Edward O. *The Meaning of Human Existence*. Liveright. 2014.

Citations

Front matter

"I cannot conceive of a God who rewards and punishes …"
Einstein. *The World As I See It. p. 5.*

"There is a soul at the center of nature …"
Emerson. *Essays: First Series.* Spiritual Laws.

Introduction

"A religion … that stressed the magnificence of the universe …"
Sagan. *Pale Blue Dot.* p. 50.

"In our best times everything turns into religion …"
Muir. *My First Summer in the Sierra.* September 7.

Part 1

Origins

Origins story, by Carl Sagan
Sagan. *Cosmos.* p. 337-338.

"It is not necessary to invoke God to ... set the Universe going."
Hawking and Mlodinow. *The Grand Design*. p. 180.

"We are star-stuff pondering the stars!"
Sagan. *Cosmos*. p. 345.

Ways of the world

"In the new world view, the universe is seen ..."
Capra, *The Tao of Physics*. p. 286.

"Emergence is about new realities ..."
Rue. *Nature is Enough*. p. 74.

"the force of electric attraction ..."
Capra. *The Tao of Physics*. p. 72.

"the activity of matter is the very essence of its being ..."
Capra. *The Tao of Physics*. p. 203.

some embrace acknowledgment of mystery
Goodenough. "My covenant with mystery."

Life

"If you put effort into understanding what life is ..."
Fleischman. p. 150.

"When we look at the world around us, we find that we are ..."
Capra. *The Hidden Connections*. p. 69.

Being Human

"Know thyself"
Pausanias. *Description of Greece*.

"Only wisdom based on self-understanding … will save us."
E.O. Wilson. *The Meaning of Human Existence*. p. 15.

"The question of interest is no longer whether …"
E.O. Wilson. *Human Nature*. p. 18.

Universal Human Qualities
Pinker. *The Blank Slate*. p. 435-438.

Behaviors/Customs Present in all Cultures
Wilson. *On Human Nature*. p. 22.
(compiled by George P. Murdock in 1945)

"free will" is different and less free than is widely assumed
Dennett. *Elbow Room* and Goodenough "Who Is My I Self?"

much of what we "feel" when we are anxious …
Damasio. p. 59-62.

"Automatic processes run the human mind …"
Haidt. p. 45.

atheists answered that these were "meant to be"
Bering & Heywood. p. 32.

as many as 50%… "religious or spiritual awakening."
Pew Research Center. "Religious and Mystical Experiences."

some studies of meditation have shown …
PBS. "Religion and the Brain." 4:35-5:25.

Being religious

"Why bother about spirituality?"
Stone. "Spirituality for Naturalists." p. 499.

"a meaning, or an enchantment and glory …"
James. *Varieties of Religious Experience*. Lecture XX.

"there are religious aspects of this world ..."
Stone. *Religious Naturalism Today*. p. 1.

One perspective on what it can mean to be religious ...
Rue. *Religion Is Not About God*. p. 127-129.

a potential future "Ecozoic Era"
Berry. "The Ecozoic Era"

Part of the challenge was discussed by E. O. Wilson ...
Wilson. *The Meaning of Human Existence*. p. 174-176.

... a religious naturalist "takes nature to heart."
Rue. *Nature Is Enough*. p. 110.

"the gratitude and astonishment of being alive."
Goodenough. "Are You A Religious Naturalist ...?"

"a larger, richer, more satisfying life ..."
James. *The Varieties of Religious Experience*. Lecture XX.

"He who knows it not and can no longer wonder ..."
Einstein. *The World As I See It*. p. 5.

"It was the experience of mystery – even if mixed with fear ..."
Einstein. *The World As I See It*. p. 5.

Part 2

"So now we can talk practices..."
Phares. Recorded sermon. 12:32-13:06.

This range of options is similar to Hinduism ...
Rue. *Nature is Enough*. p. 135.

With parallels to aspects of Japanese Shinto tradition ...
Encyclopaedia Britannica. Shinto. Ritual Practices and Institutions.

Practices that orient the mind

"These experiences lift us up out of our narrow selves ..."
Idler. p. 1.

sacred time
Idler. p. 4. (sacred/profane, as discussed by Emile Durkheim)

Encounters with nature

the power of the slowing
May. Chapter 2.

biophilia
Wilson. *Biophilia.*

nature deficit disorder
Louv. *Last Child in the Woods.* p. 36.

a scientifically informed mindfulness
Barrett essay. (quoting and discussing Braxton, 2007)

Encounters with art

"When a play or production works ..."
Brown, Lenora Inez. p. 27.

"We dance ... to disappear in something bigger ..."
Roth. p. 1.

Other practices

"just become aware of your breath ..."
Fitzpatrick. p. 86. (quoting Thich Nhat Hanh)

Transcendental meditation ... in medical studies
Benson. *The Relaxation Response.* p. 71-72.

"responding to events or mysteries that we cannot fathom"
Moore. *A Religion of One's Own*. p. 5

the Cosmic Walk
Deeptime Network. *The Cosmic Walk webpage*.

Michael Dowd and Connie Barlow - activities with children
Dowd and Barlow. Great Story Beads webpage.

before drinking a glass of water, we might stop and reflect
Crosby. *More Than Discourse*. p. 91.

Spiritual growth or transformation

"Spiritual practice is a process of spiritual transformation…"
Strain. p. 355.

"To let go of unworthy attachments, the old Self has to 'die'…"
McNamara. p. 147.

Developing religious attitudes

"Religion means much more than a state of mind …"
PBS. "Religion and the Brain." 2:57-3:07.

"Compassion is a practically acquired knowledge, like dancing…"
Eng. Q&A with Karen Armstrong.

Seeking knowledge and wisdom

"The further the spiritual evolution of mankind advances …"
Einstein. *Ideas and Opinions*. p. 53.

"unweaving the rainbow"
Dawkins. p. ix-xii.

Community

"People deeply need membership in a group"
Wilson. *The Meaning of Human Existence*. p. 150.

Putting Values into Practice

"Surely it is the way a person lives and practices ..."
Davies, p. 55.

"Although spiritual social activists ... certainly want to win ..."
Gottlieb. p. 193.

Part 3

Natural sense of self

"There is no little man sitting in the mind somewhere ..."
McNamara. p. 27.
Graphic
Adapted from an image (Cartesian Theater) created by Jennifer Garcia
Provided via WikiCommons
https://creativecommons.org/licenses/by-sa/2.5/legalcode

"The child is father of the man"
From "My Heart Leaps Up" by William Wordsworth. 1802.

as was discussed in *The Tao of Physics* ...
Capra. *The Tao of Physics*. p. 11, 24-25.

Nature as a Focus of Religious Orientation

"The problem with nature being considered …"
    Crosby. *Living with Ambiguity*. p. 12.

"Should we worship the morally ambiguous?"
    Stone. "What is Religious Naturalism?" p. 71.

Envisioning nature

"The Tao gives rise to all forms …"
    Walker. p. 8.

"The universe is no longer a mere It to us …"
    James. *The Will to Believe*. X.

Taking guidance from the natural world

"A central task of culture should be to remind us …"
    School of Nature. Chapter 5.

"Nothing in the world is as soft and yielding as water."
    Mitchell. *Tao Te Ching*. #78. p. 79.

As in the quote from Karl Peters, below …
    Peters. *Dancing with the Sacred*. P. 111-112.

Natural values and morality

"Is that which the gods love good because they love it …"
    Plato, Euthyphro

"We want to understand how best to be good."
    Goodenough and Woodruff. p. 586.

"a few themes keep popping up …"
    Pinker. "The Moral Instinct." p. 7/14.

a difference between religion and education
de Botton. 6:05.

Finding Hope, Strength, and Meaning

"Every viable system of religious beliefs and practices ..."
Crosby. *Living with Ambiguity*. page 91.

Purpose and meaning

"The more the universe seems comprehensible ..."
Weinberg. p. 154.

"Things do not matter in and of themselves ..."
Comte-Sponville. p. 203-204.

a "credo of continuation"
Goodenough. *The Sacred Depths of Nature*. p. 171.

by giving, we receive.
McDonnell. *Psychology Today*.

"the meaning of life differs from man to man ..."
Frankl. p. 130-131.

"What was really needed was a fundamental change ..."
Frankl. p. 98.

"Is there a courage which can conquer the anxiety ..."
Tillich. *The Courage to Be*. p. 174.

"The act of accepting meaninglessness ..."
Tillich. *The Courage to Be*. p. 176.

"A man who becomes conscious of the responsibility ..."
Frankl. p. 101.

Alienation

"I am a forty-two-year-old woman…"
Keen. p. 72.

"We belong to the universe, we are at home in it …"
Capra. *The Hidden Connections*. p. 69.

"I had the sense that I was intimately connected to everything …"
Newberg and Waldman. p. 215.

In a Pew survey, about half of all respondents …
Pew Research Center. p. 12.

Michael Hogue described how we can see ourselves …
Hogue. p. xv-xvi.

Mortality

"In moments of grief – deep grief – the only consolation …"
Rojas. p. 1.

Ursula Goodenough gave an explanation
Goodenough. *The Sacred Depths of Nature*. p. 143-149.

"And it is here that we arrive …"
Goodenough. *The Sacred Depths of Nature*. p. 149.

the "butterfly effect"
Vernon. p. 130.

"a serenity is on offer …"
Goodenough. IRASnet.

"The secret of the enjoyment of pleasure …"
Watts, p. 53.

Personal Religious Orientation

"Different people are religious in different ways."
  Schlauch. p. 5.

God language

"I cannot conceive of a God who rewards and punishes …"
  Einstein. *The World As I See It.* p. 5.

Some use God as Stuart Kauffman did (as a symbol …)
  Kauffman. "Beyond Reductionism"

…as Paul Tillich did (as "ground of being")
  Tillich. *Systematic Theology Volume I.* p. 239.

… as Nancy Abrams describes – as a symbol …
  Abrams. Chapter 3.

Religious Identity

religious aspects … appreciated within a naturalistic framework
  Stone. *Religious Naturalism Today.* p. 1.

a lifestance "guided by reason, inspired by compassion …"
  American Humanist Association. Introduction.

Wrap-up

"There will be a new church founded on moral science …"
  Emerson. *Essays: First Series.* Worship.

"After you have exhausted what there is …"
  Whitman. "Specimen Days."

Appendix

Being Religious – Quotes

"We come to life in this world …"
　Wildman. p. 17.

"… religion is a way of life that involves many processes …"
　Streng et al. p. 6.

"A religious person … may or may not self-identify …"
　Goodenough and Deacon. p. 865.

"If you have ever extended a simple kindness …"
　Gottlieb. p. 13.

"Spirituality begins in movement …"
　Gottlieb. p. 7.

"As taught by virtually every religious tradition …"
　Gottlieb. p. 9.

"The important difference between religious (spiritual)…"
　Rue. *Nature is Enough*. p. 110.

"Typical of religious outlooks and experiences …"
　Crosby. *The Thou of Nature*. p. 52.

"The religious attitude … accepts the objective truth …"
　Dworkin. p. 10.

"There are countless … ways in which …"
　Gottlieb. p. 13.

"William James said that: Like love, like wrath …"
　Dworkin. p. 11.

"The universe is no longer a mere It to us, it is a Thou …"
James. *The Varieties of Religious Experience*. Lecture XX.

"the religious sensibility opens up an … inspiring vision …"
Crosby. *The Thou of Nature*. p. 126.

"Were one asked to characterize the life of religion …"
James. *The Varieties of Religious Experience*. Lecture XX.

"Religion means much more than a state of mind …"
PBS. "Religion and the Brain." 2:57-3:07.

"… to borrow a phrase from Jesus of Nazareth …"
Dark. p. 22.

"I am religious precisely because …"
Simonton. p. 1.

Printed in Great Britain
by Amazon